HOW TO PREPARE
FOR DEATH

HOW TO
PREPARE FOR DEATH

A Practical Guide

by Yaffa Draznin

HAWTHORN BOOKS, INC.

Publishers/NEW YORK

Library of Congress Catalog Card Number: 75-41804

ISBN: 0-8015-3736-3

1 2 3 4 5 6 7 8 9 10

Contents

Preface   vii

PART I

Preparing for Your Own Death

1. The Preliminaries   3
2. Disposing of the Body   8
3. The Mortuary Rite   22
4. Costs—and "A Fitting Funeral"   30
5. Arranging the Funeral and Burial   40
6. Paying the Funeral and Cemetery Costs   53
7. Disposing of Your Worldly Possessions: The Will   63
8. Providing a Financial Cushion: Insurance   75
9. Providing a Financial Cushion: Estate Conservation   85

PART II

Special Decisions When Death Is Imminent

10. *Preparation for Your Own Death*   97
11. *Preparing for a Death in the Family*   105

PART III

Coping with a Death in the Family

12. *Death as It Really Is*   113
13. *The Expected Death: Immediate Steps*   116
14. *The Sudden Accidental Death: Immediate Steps*   123
15. *The Suicide and Homicide: Immediate Steps*   138
16. *Making Arrangements for the Funeral and Burial*   145
17. *Arranging to Pay the Funeral and Burial Costs*   155
18. *Actual Burial/Cremation Rites and Procedures*   164
19. *Immediate Postdeath Arrangements*   177
20. *Settling the Small Estate*   190
21. *The Large Estate and Executor Duties*   196

    Epilogue   207
    Supplemental Reading Notes   209
    Index   217

Preface

This is a book about the secular problems of death, dealing with such mundane matters as funeral and burial arrangements, insurance and social security allotments, wills. Compared to the tidal wave of concern about the emotional and psychological ramifications of death, interest in such pragmatic matters seems to stir hardly a ripple of concern.

But in all other areas, enthusiasm is rampant. What ten years ago was a trickle and in 1970 a healthy stream, by 1976 has become a bibliographic torrent of major proportions. Death has become our prime nonfictional fascination.

Theologians and the spiritually minded have explored the Mystery of Death in depth, based on personal and pastoral experiences. Psychologists, psychiatrists, and social workers have dissected the myriad emotional problems of death: the denial of death, the trauma of facing death, the grief syndrome when death takes place, personal adjustments occurring during bereavement. Sociologists and anthropologists, psychologists and therapists are even now carrying out research projects in such quantity and of such complexity that

Dr. Robert Slater has predicted sociologists of the future "will look back at the 1970s and say it was the decade of Death, just as the '50s was the decade of Sex, and the '60s of Drugs."

I would like to suggest that much of this energy is misdirected. The trauma surrounding death seems to have a much more pragmatic base. The bereaved are often less in need of a clergyman or a social worker than they are of the services of a good tax accountant, a forceful insurance agent, or someone to do hardheaded bargaining with the mortician. The fear of being left without any source of income is enough to cause panic of major proportions. The tension of being involved in a court battle with one's own children over a will, the shock of being a victim of a fraudulent cemetery scheme, the impossible strain of talking money and bargaining about funeral arrangements the day after a death in the family—these tensions are not just incidental to the trauma. They *are* the trauma.

This book addresses itself to the consideration of these death-related problems. In the following pages death is viewed as a secular event that produces a number of society-linked problems on which decisions have to be made. The decisions are usually financial and legal. Some are commercial, involving the purchase of goods and services. But even when the goods and services involved are caskets, cemetery lots, and funeral arrangements, the decisions are not unlike the ones a person regularly makes every day.

Sometimes these decisions involve options and alternatives. When they do, the specific choices to be made are like other choices we make under similar circumstances and pressures. And if the decisions happen to relate to an event in the future, they are still no different than other contingency plans for the future. Facts must be gathered, alternatives considered, choices made, and, as time goes by, past decisions reviewed and altered. This book explains how to do these things where death is concerned.

Let me stress what this book is *not* about. It is not concerned with the Mystery of Death, although a basic assumption is that a quick and equitable solution to many of these society-linked problems makes a tranquil confrontation with death much easier. It's not an exposé of the "extravagances of the maudlin deception" of the funeral industry, although in context much will be said about funeral costs and practices. Nor will it deal with the problems of dying—a totally different subject—except briefly in the section about special decisions when an illness is terminal. In addition, there is little here on grief or bereavement, although the influences of both on an ability to cope will be taken into consideration.

The book is divided into three parts: Part I, "Preparing for Your Own Death"; Part II, an interstitial section, "Special Decisions When Death Is Imminent"; and Part III, "Coping with a Death in the Family."

While the first half of the book appears to cover the same ground as the second half (disposing of the body, transferring property, providing a financial cushion), the "point of view," as novelists use the term, is altogether different. This makes the consideration of the problems a difference of substance, not just direction.

Person A who prepares for his or her own death is not the same person as Person B who must cope with the problems caused by the death of Person A. The will-maker is not the same person as that will's beneficiary. The man or woman who purchases life insurance has altogether different objectives than the man or woman who cashes in that insurance policy. *Choosing* an executor is not the same as *being* an executor.

Moreover, the many options available to Person A and the

lengthy time available for making decisions, make the problems to be faced different in kind, not just degree, from the problems that Person B faces. A principal preparing for his or her own death (that *you* of Part I) plans for an event that will take place in an indefinite future. The choices are many and varied; you have time to think them over carefully, with deliberation. Whether you decide in favor of one or another, there is no permanent change in your life, or anyone else's, for the moment. The choices are still revokable.

In Part III, death is an accomplished fact. *You* in Part III are the survivor whose choices are few *and* limited. Deliberate thinking is out of the question because time pressure is very real. All choices previously made by someone else are now irrevocable, binding upon you, no matter how altered the circumstances from when the choices were originally made.

For the *you* in Part III, everything has changed. Your life is completely disrupted; entirely new relationships must form. Where before you were a dependent, now you're the head of a household with others dependent on you. Where before you were encumbered, now suddenly you're independent of all responsibilities. Before you may have been rather poor—now suddenly you've a large sum of insurance money at your disposal. The new, still unstable, situation is quite different from the settled time when the decisions were made by the principal of Part I.

Yet all three parts are linked under a single, overall umbrella: They are all survivor-oriented. The problems discussed in this book are society-related problems. And while it appears self-evident, we tend to forget that only those who are living when the problems occur are concerned with their solutions. When we talk about death (not *dying*, but *death*), only the survivors are involved.

Much of the information in this book is expert opinion

gleaned from voluminous printed matter, from correspondence, and from personal interviews. A lot is expert only in the sense of personal experience, information volunteered by survivors who related what happened when the death in their family occurred: what they did initially and then, afterwards, how they made the funeral arrangements and paid for them, what kind of insurance they were left and how they made claim for the money, whether there was a will and how it affected them, and so on. These lay interviews helped put the other expert opinion into human perspective.

In the egalitarian democracy of alphabetical order, I'd like to acknowledge some of those who gave time and thought to my project: Ralph Bailey, Larry Boland, Elsie Bolton, Fred Drake, Morton Effron, Ricardo Gutierrez, Paul Hultquist, Allace Kunz, Fred Lacey, Ruth Levin, Barbara Walton.

For the rest of the material here, its organization and judgments, I must take personal responsibility. If there are factual errors, I trust they are minor; I've tried to be as accurate as possible. If there are opinions that some object to, I'm sorry; not for the opinions, but that people should take umbrage. And if any of the perceptions and helpful hints are valid, I'm glad. It may make the job of coping with death easier for us all.

PART I

Preparing for Your Own Death

I

The Preliminaries

Human society everywhere, all over the globe and back into history, has established certain cultural norms around the imperatives of death. The requirements are few but unvarying. The corpse must be taken care of, the dead given a new status and the solidarity of the group reaffirmed, the deceased's property distributed among those who remain, and the bereaved comforted and reestablished in society without the deceased.

Cultural norms change but the imperatives remain the same. In America today, when someone dies we hold some kind of funeral ritual, both to recognize that a viable member of the group is now gone and to reaffirm that the society as a whole remains; then we bury or cremate the body, redistribute the property, and help the survivors reestablish themselves in the world without the one who died.

One of the characteristics of our culture is that we also provide the instruments to permit an individual to take care of these death imperatives in anticipation of his or her *own* death. Through wills, trusts, insurance, and prearranged funeral plans one can plan ahead so as to alleviate much of the grief and dislocation that death will cause the survivors.

Most of us feel that this kind of planning for death is important. In a recent survey, when adult Americans were asked about different ways to adjust to life's uncertainty, 85 percent agreed that "people should try to make plans about death." And fully half the number in the survey had already talked with those closest to them about doing something.

But what we say and what we actually do are often quite different. Only 24 percent, less than one-fourth of us, have executed a will, and just a fraction more, 28 percent of the total, have made any funeral or cemetery arrangements. This unwillingness to do anything about what we know is inevitable reflects an obvious ambivalence toward death.

Experts differ as to why we drag our feet so. Some attribute this to the feeling that making practical arrangements about death profanes the sacred aura around the Mystery of Death. Others give it a more irrational, superstitious cast: the belief that thinking and planning for death somehow brings death about sooner than it would otherwise happen.

Some ecclesiastics see a death-avoidance ruse in our idolizing of the huge advances of medical science, where death appears to be simply an accident that might be avoided through better health habits and the discovery of a new antibiotic. One social scientist has said that the recently articulated resentment against the ripoffs of the funeral industry has been seized upon by many as providing socially approved reasons to avoid doing what they unconsciously didn't want to do in the first place.

Yet against all these rationalizations is the admitted certainty that if we don't make plans, our survivors must make them for us; and for them it is a very traumatic, usually costly, certainly frightening experience. We want to prevent this if we can.

Perhaps we can. Perhaps it's just a matter of approach. This chapter and the next eight are devoted to developing how this can be done.

BRINGING THE MATTER INTO THE OPEN

Remove death from the list of unmentionable conversational subjects by talking openly and frankly about funeral plans and making a will. Bring it up among friends or at a social gathering. Sometimes a discussion group can be deliberately set up for this purpose at your club or church. Once the question is broached (though you can expect a ritualized denial that it's of any interest and certainly much ribald humor) you'll be amazed to find out how many people are eager to exchange views and ideas on the subject. Friends recently through a bereavement often are eager to tell what they *should* have done (instead of what they did do) so others can benefit from their mistakes. Lawyers and insurance agents who repeatedly deal with death-related problems have many experiences to relate. A judge may be able to tell of probate court work, explaining what happens and how its problems can be lessened. Ministers with repeated encounters with the families of the terminally ill often know too well what difficulties a lack of preparation can cause.

INCLUDE YOUR NEXT OF KIN IN THE DISCUSSION AND PLANNING

If you are married, try to bring your spouse into the discussion. The same applies if you are a single adult living with a friend. You might be startled to find out he or she often has thought about the subject but was afraid to mention it to you for fear you might find him or her too morbid.

EXPLORE GENERAL QUESTIONS AT THE OUTSET

There are some broad matters you may want to broach at the beginning (and the *you* in this context means two of you or all of you). The questions are hypothetical but important, and talking about them helps desensitize a sensitive subject. Suppose one of you should die?—what should the other do?

Try to imagine the situation as occurring in the next few months. Think about it, even though it makes you a little anxious. Should the survivor stay where he or she is and live alone? Or go live with children, another relative, or a friend? Should the move be to a retirement home where there are other older, active, but slightly dependent singles? Suppose the survivor has to earn a living: How would either of you go about it? Is remarriage the answer? Would a change of job or orientation be feasible at this age?

Talking about these matters will open up a closed area. As you think of them for a while and then return to the subject you'll find it easier to consider more specific death-related problems.

DISCUSS SPECIFIC PLANS TOGETHER

Now pass on to a discussion of what should be done about funeral and burial arrangements. Perhaps you're in accord and have taken care of the matter already, with no question as to what you want.

In any case, talk it out so there is no doubt about your feelings on the subject. Don't keep it a secret if you've already made any arrangements, no matter how kindly your motives.

It's senseless to keep others in the dark about your plans or wishes; they're the ones who will have to carry them out at your death.

Making it a joint affair makes sense for another reason. Capricious fate being what it is, there is no guarantee that death will come in chronological or mortality-table order. You may end up carrying out someone else's wishes rather than vice versa.

If there's a difference of opinion, this is the time to air it. If not cleared up now, a family squabble is certain to arise later, should any member of the family wish to disregard instructions that another wants to honor.

But before you make up your mind, be sure you are aware of all of the facts and alternatives regarding funeral and burial. The following chapters review them in detail.

2

Disposing of the Body

The many "policy" questions regarding the disposition of the body cover a whole series of decisions. Should it be a traditional earth burial? Or should it be cremation? Or do you prefer to have your body or parts of it donated to medical science? Do you want a funeral service? Should there be open-casket viewing of the body? Or should the casket be closed? Would a memorial service without the body present be more "fitting"? How much ceremony *is* fitting? Is the cost of the funeral relevant? If so, how much money should be spent on these final rites?

These questions suggest alternatives in mortuary rites and modes, some of which you may not have considered. Mull them over now, evaluate the options with deliberation, talk about them with others to find out what they think. Do this particularly when you are in good health. When you're ill is hardly the time to consider alternative funeral and burial arrangements.

Consider the advantages and disadvantages of all the options you have to find those that match your way of life, your mode of thinking, your outward wishes, and your inner needs. But whatever decision you arrive at now, don't consider the matter disposed of once and for all. Your perspective on the various alternatives changes over the years as you get older and your financial condition, religious commitment, and social status change. Once-made decisions should be reviewed regularly and altered as your values change.

Remember, *disposition of the remains is not the same as mortuary rites.* These are two separate matters calling for two or more separate decisions. The first is what to do with the actual body; that is, should it be buried or cremated? The second is what kind of religious rite—if any—should accompany the disposition.

Many people frequently confuse and amalgamate the two. Some people, for example, tend to equate expensive, ostentatious funerals with burial and low-cost simplicity with cremation. This is not necessarily true. Some individuals opt for cremation and yet insist on elaborate and costly funerals and very expensive viewable niches for the inurnment of the remains. On the other hand, some religious sects bury and memorialize their own dead; for them burial is a simple and inexpensive process.

It's necessary to keep a perspective on any discussion of burial or cremation. At the moment, the burial versus cremation controversy is a much-discussed topic in the printed media and perhaps on college campuses; but, in fact, at present the matter is not a real issue, except possibly in the Far West. The use of cremation in preference to burial is still very much in its infancy, used in only about 6.2 percent of all deaths. However, considering the rapidity of change in America, cremation might suddenly attract great numbers of new adherents, many new crematories might be built across the nation, and within a few years the use of cremation might find heretofore unknown public acceptance. This is why considering all possibilities is very important now.

In American society only two alternatives for disposing of the body are available for all practical purposes: burial (either above or below the ground) and cremation.

A third possibility, burial at sea, is done only in very special circumstances: when death takes place on the high seas with no facilities on board to refrigerate the body until port is reached; during war when military personnel on board are killed; or by specific testamentary request of active or retired Navy personnel.

Another possibility often suggested as an alternative method of disposition, donating one's body to science, is actually just an intermediate step. After the medical school has completed its use of the cadaver, the remains must still be cremated or buried by the school or the family to whom it is returned. However, because the family who contributes the body often regards bequeathal as final disposition, this method will be discussed later as another alternative.

BURIAL VERSUS CREMATION

Because burial and cremation are the major methods of disposition available, comparisons of the two often become antagonistic when support of one deteriorates into simple condemnation of the other. It is particularly difficult to separate advocacy from denunciation when both are part of the same argument.

A more difficult problem to resolve is that advocates of each often argue from different sets of premises. Many of the arguments advanced for burial, for example, are real but intangible, such as the overwhelming preference of many religious faiths for its use as compared to cremation. Arguments for cremation, on the other hand, tend to be real and *very* tangible, such as the matter of cost.

Burial advocates address themselves (as do those who favor the traditional funeral) to the religious, nonrational needs they feel must be satisfied at time of death. Their appeal in modern terms is to the psychiatric findings that point to unconscious needs. They are less concerned with appeals to reason.

On the other hand, advocates of immediate cremation (and often those who prefer a memorial service without viewing) advance logical, rational, secular arguments that have a sensible appeal for those who feel them valid. The pro-cremation forces counter assertions of nonrational needs with rational denials.

It's a matter of comparing noncompatibles. As long as one understands that we're presenting positions that cannot be itemized neatly in two opposing columns schoolroom fashion, we can gather the material and opinions available for an overview of the subject.

HISTORICAL PERSPECTIVES

Burial and cremation are both very ancient customs, dating from prehistoric times. Archeological evidence shows the burial of bodies goes back at least 70,000 years. There is also evidence of cremation being practiced in the Stone Age in Eastern Europe and the Near East, spreading across northern Europe, and probably coming to the British Isles from Britanny in the early Bronze Age.

The spread of cremation throughout the ancient world was rather general. Only a few cultures resisted the practice: The Egyptians developed the preservation of the body by embalming; the Chinese buried their dead; and the Jews changed from cave and sepulchre to earth burial.

In Greece, the practice of cremation entered the culture about 1000 B.C. It had become the prevalent method of disposition by the Homeric period, and the Romans, in turn, quite possibly received the custom from them.

In contrast to the Greeks and the Romans, the ancient Jews rarely employed cremation. The Semitic people brought burial into the land of the pre-Canaanites about 2500 B.C., where cremation had been practiced before. The Old Testament shows that burial was by far the strongly accepted practice.

The early Christians continued the preference and practice of Judaism, although there seems to have been no clearcut reasons why cremation was resisted. Some Christian historians say this was stimulated more as a political reaction to pagan supporters of cremation than by theological arguments against the practice inherent in the Christian faith.

By the fifth century A.D. burial had totally superseded cremation throughout the Christian world. This exclusive preference continued into the nineteenth century, when the modern cremation movement got underway.

In the middle and late nineteenth century, European interest in cremation revived for both sanitary and medical reasons. The Cremation Society of England was organized by Queen Victoria's surgeon in 1874. The first modern crematory was built in Germany in 1879. In 1902, England passed its first law permitting cremation, although it had been practiced for the previous eighteen years without interference. By World War II, widespread development of municipal crematories had made the practice prevalent in the British Isles. Today cremation accounts for 60 percent of all the dispositions there.

In America sentiment for cremation arose about the same time as it did in Western Europe. The first American crematory was built in 1876, and the New York Cremation

Society was founded in 1881. In 1913, the Cremation Society of America was formed.

However, unlike Great Britain and elsewhere in northwestern Europe, the practice has not grown in America with any rapidity. Although there has been an acceleration within the last five years, the most generous estimate of the annual number of cremations in the United States as of 1974 stood at 6.2 percent of all deaths—only 1.7 percentage points greater than twenty years ago.

DESCRIPTION

Earth burial, entombment (burial above the ground), and cremation are now confined to authorized cemeteries or cemetery areas (with rare exceptions).

In earth burial the body is placed in a coffin or casket and buried in a plot of ground, the area of ground and depth of burial varying in America with time, place, and cemetery custom. The caskets of bodies that are entombed are placed in shelters known as mausoleums. These vary in size, housing a solitary casket, six to twelve caskets of a single family, or numerous crypts in one building, usually two to three stories high (although one in Nashville, Tennessee, is twenty stories high). In states with warm climates, such as California, Florida, and Texas, there are also garden mausoleums, consisting of an unroofed honeycomb-like structure of crypts out in the open.

In cremation the body is placed in a suitable container or casket and put into a specially designed furnace which reduces the body in several hours to a residue of ash and small bone fragments. The cremated ashes or remains are then disposed of in various ways: by scattering on the land or into streams or the sea; by burial within a cemetery or on private property; or stored privately or in a closed building near the crematory (community vaultage). The ashes can also be placed in an urn in a niche inside a building called a columbarium. Which alternative is chosen depends on the wishes of the closest next of kin and the legal restrictions of the various states.

Of the two disposal methods, burial is by all counts the most commonly practiced in the United States, accounting for 93.8 percent of all deaths. The figure varies greatly from state to state. In California this burial figure drops to about 70 percent; in Kansas, the figure is nearly 100 percent.

ARGUMENTS FOR BURIAL

Proponents of traditional burial argue that burial is a familiar and common method of disposal, one approved of by all one's friends, family, and co-religionists, supplying many powerful and positive emotional and cultural supports.

By far the strongest argument in favor of burial is the fact that many dominant religious bodies in America approve of it as the *only* method, while others support it overwhelmingly, even while permitting cremation for those of the faith who wish it. While Judeo-Christian institutions that endorsed burial exclusively in the past recently softened their official anti-cremation stand, the influence of tradition remains very strong.

The Eastern Orthodox churches forbid cremation for their followers. So do such Protestant churches as the Missouri Synod of the Lutheran Church, the Evangelical churches, and other fundamentalist sects. Islam, whose tradition teaches that the dead body is fully conscious of pain, strictly forbids cremation; its precepts are binding on the Black Muslims in America.

Orthodox Judaism not only forbids cremation but entombment as well, sanctioning only earth burial for members of the faith. Conservative Judaism does not strictly forbid cremation but nonetheless strongly supports the Orthodox position of requiring earth burial.

The Roman Catholic Church, long staunchly against cremation, has recently revised its stand with the lifting of the ban by the Second Vatican Council in 1963. Cremation is now permitted under certain conditions and circumstances, but it still is not an alternative to be chosen at individual discretion. Roman Catholics who wish to be cremated must request specific permission from the chancery office of their diocese. Despite the Roman Catholic Church's more permissive stance in America, the Church still advocates burial as the preferred method of disposal.

The Mormon church in America leaves it up to every family, but cremation is definitely discouraged.

The Protestant churches vary in their position of support and advocacy. The traditionalist denominations that categorically oppose cremation do so on fundamentalist grounds, seeing the practice unsanctioned by the Bible, historically anti-Christian, and defeating the literal bodily resurrection.

Other conservative Protestant denominations, while not specifically forbidding cremation, strongly discourage it although individual ministers may openly favor the practice.

ARGUMENTS FOR CREMATION

In the same way that burial advocates denounce cremation, arguments for cremation often are more anti-burial than pro-cremation. One very vocal argument in favor of cremation has been cost, expressed as a denunciation of the high cost of burial. Pointing to its relative economy as compared to burial (which requires embalming, an expensive casket, a cemetery lot, the cost of opening and closing the grave, and a memorial stone or marker), the argument has validity.

Many who use this argument admit, in good faith, that the money savings are real *only* if the body is cremated immediately after death, without funeral or committal services, and with no burial or inurnment of the remains. Otherwise these attendant expenses make the cost factor much less favorable.

The writers of popular exposés of the funeral industry have documented in detail the extent to which burial is becoming more and more a comparatively expensive indulgence. Their findings have been supported by recent corroborative data gathered by both private and governmental bodies that show how enormously the cost of burial has risen over the past twenty years.

Some spokesmen for the memorial society movement (who support immediate cremation followed by a memorial service) tend to downplay the cost argument, choosing to stress simplicity and dignity rather than dollars and cents as the measure of their position. Others, however, do press the cost argument, often incorrectly, by linking their support for cremation to a preference for simplicity as against extravagance. This is more an argument against the ritual and customary practices of the traditional American funeral than against burial.

There are many clerical supporters of cremation in America. The majority of the main-stream Protestant churches of America accept cremation when it is the expressed preference of the parishioner. The stand of the Episcopal church in support of the practice has been influenced by the position of the Church of England, which actively sanctions it. Similarly, the American clergy of those religious denominations active in countries where cremation is normative also take a positive stance for cremation for their American parishioners.

Reform Judaism, the most liberal branch of Judaism, is in general receptive to cremation, finding it as legitimate as burial if the member wishes it. Christian Scientists are either buried or cremated: This is not a doctrinal question for them.

The Unitarian/Universalist church is strongly procremation for both rational and philosophic reasons. Members of the Unitarian church have often been in the forefront of the memorial society movement that strongly comes out for immediate cremation.

Clerical supporters of cremation use the theological arguments that God would hardly have any more difficulty resurrecting cremated bodies than He would those that have rotted away into the ground; nor would He deny Eternal Life to the martyrs who died by fire in anti-Christian hands. Individual pastors also advance the behaviorist argument that religious mores often follow secular changes in opinion. They point out that in those countries where cremation has been largely accepted for pragmatic or ecological reasons, Christian leaders who formerly opposed the practice now welcome and support it.

Individual pastors and laymen often support cremation on aesthetic or spiritual grounds. One widely distributed lay account, written in 1937 and reprinted by a high-circulation magazine at regular intervals since, extols the process as aesthetically rewarding, seeing the body as enveloped "in light, like the sun." Others find it a vehicle that permits a more sensitive contemplation of the Mystery of Death, "quickly doing away with the body so that all attention may be devoted to the spirit."

Most of the cremation arguments are secular ones, and there are many of them. Ernest Morgan, speaking for the memorial society movement in his *A Manual of Death Education and Simple Burial*, states: "Modern cremation is a clean, orderly process for returning human remains to the elements. . . . The ashes (actually pulverized bone fragments) are clean and white and may be stored indefinitely or mailed by parcel post for distant interment."

Others stress the value of cremation's frugal use of land although the argument is commonly expressed in anti-burial terms by decrying the use of land "for the dead" (i.e., for cemeteries) rather than being used "for the living" (i.e., for anything but cemeteries). Some also urge the multiple use of present cemeteries for parks and playgrounds, and oppose the perpetual and exclusive use of such land for burial. The ecological argument that America is heading toward a land shortage similar to England, Holland, Switzerland, and Japan is also advanced.

Because burial is regarded as the traditional method and cremation as more modern, one of the strong arguments advanced for cremation is its very nonconformity, its antiestablishment character. According to Rev. Paul Irion in his book *Cremation*, this characterization should not be interpreted as invidious condemnation of the supporters of cremation. Many people, says Dr. Irion, choose to make up their minds on important subjects without concerning themselves as to whether or not they deviate from the more established pattern. Those who pride themselves in doing what they themselves (and presumably their closest next of kin) approve of, find opting for cremation is a means of expressing this independence.

This overall view of the burial/cremation sentiments hardly pretends to cover all the pros and cons of the controversy. Most of the arguments for cremation are rational and progressive; the counterarguments for burial are religious and traditional. Which of the two is the more spiritually uplifting (if that's what one wants) and psychologically supportive of the bereaved is a matter of widely differing expert opinion. But the use of each is so often linked to the mortuary rites that accompany it that these, which are discussed in the following chapter, must also be considered before a decision can be made.

DONATING ONE'S BODY TO MEDICAL SCIENCE

Presenting one's body, wholly or in part, as a gift to a medical school after death is an alternative that has received a great deal of publicity in the media recently, and the idea of "permitting the dead to serve the living" is a very appealing one. The Uniform Anatomical Gift Act (or its equivalent), which has been adopted in all fifty states, permits individuals to bequeath their bodies for immediate use after death by medical schools or hospitals, without requiring permission of the closest next of kin. But there are a number of rather complicated steps involved. Without prejudicing the case for such a move, *make sure you read the fine print first.* You must be very careful *not* to look at this method as simply an easy way to avoid the cost of burial.

Medical schools, hospitals, schools of dentistry, and other teaching and research facilities all use cadavers for training student doctors and dentists, biology and pathology students, and research workers. But the present need for bodies and the conditions under which the schools will accept a donated body vary greatly across the country. In the Far West many schools have had so many donations that they no longer are accepting bodies. Other schools elsewhere are desperately in need of bodies, but the cost of transportation and legal restrictions prevent a more equitable nationwide distribution.

Some schools will not accept bodies that have been embalmed in any way, or on which an autopsy has been made, or which have been mutilated (as in an auto accident). Some will not accept a body from which organs have been removed for transplant. Others permit limited embalming and have less stringent rules on the body's condition. Some schools insist that they receive the body forthwith; others will give permission for a funeral service to be held before the body is transported to the medical school.

While some schools pick up the body from the hospital, others require that it be delivered to them by a licensed mortician. Some accept it without cost to the next of kin; other schools charge the full amount of the Social Security lump-sum death benefit ($255) plus the cost of transportation. Some schools require advance filing of a certificate of bequeathal, signed both by the donor and by the next of kin, or by the donor and two or three witnesses.

Many schools, as a matter of practical policy, will not accept the gift of a body from the closest next of kin if the donor (the person who is now dead) did not give written permission prior to death. Often they will refuse the gift if *anyone* in the family objects, even though the Uniform Anatomical Gift Act gives the closest next of kin the right to bequeath the body in the absence of any contrary prohibition from the person while alive.

In the other direction, many schools will refuse to accept a body if the next of kin objects, even if the donor had signed a proper instrument willing the body to the institution, as is legally required according to the Uniform Anatomical Gift Act.

The matter of donating various organs and tissues of one's body is often considered when the gift of a whole body is contemplated. Millions of persons have requested Uniform Donor Cards from various "eye banks" and organ-collection foundations throughout the country; about 10 million such cards have already been distributed, mainly through the National Kidney Foundation. The card, when properly signed and witnessed, gives blanket permission for the body to be used for parts transplants or in its entirety for any medical purpose. However, usually one must be chosen as an alternative to the other. Most medical schools cannot use a body from which any parts, except perhaps the corneas of the eyes, have been taken.

Despite popular misconceptions, there is as yet no satisfactory way of "banking" organs—of removing them and storing them until a recipient is found who can use the tissues. The transfer must be made immediately.

This means the prospective recipient of the gift organ will necessarily be present in the hospital and waiting as the donor is dying; and the blood typing, tissue matching tests, and review of the medical history all must continue to the last minute of life. According to Dr. John Najarian, chief of surgery, University of Minnesota Hospitals, the "interval of delay" between death and organ removal is approximately ten minutes. (Others say up to twelve hours is possible in cornea transplantation.) As soon as a person is pronounced dead, the body will be immediately removed and prepared for surgery. (If the next of kin is present, the fast-paced activity about the deathbed may be very traumatic.) The next of kin must later claim the body for burial or cremation after the organ removal. Hospitals that use only parts of bodies do not provide this service.

While the medical school use of a corpse has received open religious approval, some disapproval has been forthcoming from individual ministers. Some see such a use of the body as a desecration of the temple of the spirit. Others look at the donors rather than the act and term the practice antireligious since so many who choose to do it openly express anti–organized-religion views and declare themselves against the public, religion-sanctioned funeral.

3

The Mortuary Rite

Considerations of the funeral service versus the memorial service, viewing the body versus not viewing, embalming versus not embalming, although all involving separate decisions, are intertwined in the single question: What kind of mortuary rites, if any, should I have? This area frankly is so riddled with subjective value judgments and aroused feelings, many of which have little to do with the decisions involved, that only a sample of current opinion and literature can be presented here.

Anthropologists find the existence of a religious or communal rite of passage accompanying the disposal of the corpse in every society, serving "to move people from moments of personal confusion and ego impoverishment toward a restructuring of identity." As such they are ceremonials with "the basic potential for the highest order of social significance." Both the memorial service rite and the funeral rite purport to serve such a purpose in ours.

The rituals in America have varied over the years and

with particular cultural groups, but they have always been heavy with formalized, religious overtones, although these sometimes assume a strong secular expression. Today our funeral ceremony has a very distinctive and peculiarly American format. In its traditional Protestant form, it involves the embalming of the corpse and its subsequent viewing by friends and acquaintances in the funeral home before the funeral service; a religious ceremony a few days later, either in the funeral home chapel or the church; and a processional to the place of commitment where a graveside ceremony is held. The later gathering of friends at the home of the survivors for the offering of condolences is not actually part of the funeral, but generally it is understood to be associated with the mortuary rites.

The memorial service, being a very recent innovation, varies in format—there is no such thing as a traditional memorial service. The only distinguishing feature is that it is held after the body has been cremated or buried; there is no viewing of the body at any time.

The presence of the body at the traditional funeral usually involves the viewing ritual, and the embalming of the body is an intricate part of that practice in America. Embalming for open-casket viewing of the body is a method of preserving the body for a limited period by the injection of a preserving chemical into the arteries of the body. While uncommon in Europe (where it is actually rather costly and hard to come by for those who wish it done for their relatives), it is a regular practice of morticians in America, Australia, and increasingly so in England. (In England, however, cosmetics are not used as they are in America.)

Embalming is routinely done by the mortician unless the survivors specifically insist that it not be done. It is legally mandatory throughout the United States if the body is to be transported by common carrier. In some states embalming is required if there is more than a forty-eight–hour interval between death and burial or cremation.

EMBALMING OR NOT, VIEWING OR NOT

Feelings about the embalming of a body and open-casket viewing run high both among those who denounce these practices and those who defend them (although the latter use more restrained rhetoric).

Morticians who support embalming see it only as a more improved method of temporarily preserving the body (although they have been accused of misrepresenting the length of time embalming permits the body to remain intact). They insist that embalming must be done immediately and routinely when the body is received; otherwise it begins to deteriorate and changes take place rapidly. The longer embalming is delayed the harder it is to restore the flesh to the state where the features are recognizable.

Other supporters don't consider the embalming process as separate from the viewing of the body, which they feel is necessary, with real therapeutic value for the survivors.

Opponents of both see embalming with the use of cosmetics to make the body more lifelike and the viewing of the corpse as unseemly, undignified, wastefully expensive, and unnecessary.

Supporters of the open casket insist that viewing the dead body is one of the first steps in accepting reality. The presence of the dead body is "an important factor in helping the mourners to accept the fact of death, to overcome the experience of denial and to enable creative grief to take place."

In times of sudden unexpected death, according to Dr. Elizabeth Kubler-Ross, viewing is imperative in order to prevent any later denial of death that would delay working through the bereavement: "It is important that the family can view the body before the funeral in order to face the reality of the beloved one's death."

Rev. Paul Irion, a theologian who has also written about the positive aspects of cremation, believes viewing is very helpful to a bereaved family, a means "by which the whole situation is focused on reality."

But the critics of embalming find the practice offensive when coupled with the use of cosmetics to enhance the appearance of the body. One characterizes the arguments that embalming is necessary to permit open-casket viewing and that the "grief therapy" of open-casket viewing gives comfort to bereaved families as "demonstrably flimsy and ridiculous" and voices high distress that "no law presently exists to curb the specious claims of those who peddle grief therapy to the grieving." The viewing of the body is called "a theatrical production starring a theatrically made-up corpse" making "the spiritual realities as remote as any Grade-B motion picture does. . . ."

FUNERAL SERVICE OR MEMORIAL SERVICE— OR NO SERVICE

Opposition to the American funeral comes from two directions: one that would substitute a memorial service for the funeral, preferably after the body has been buried or cremated; and the other that wants to do away with all funerary rites entirely. Both positions appear to go beyond simply a desire to reduce the cost and simplify the accoutrements of funeral practice.

The organized memorial service movement, with its advocacy of "dignity, simplicity, and economy" with regard to the disposition of the body and the death rites, supports the elimination of the funeral and the viewing of the body, seeking to substitute the commemorative memorial service. Although the membership-fee organizations that comprise it put preplanning high among its purposes, the memorial service theme seems to be paramount for the majority who organize and champion the societies. "A major objective of all the societies," said one in a description of their function, "is to smooth the path of the family that prefers to hold a memorial service without the body present, instead of the 'open casket' funeral, and to guarantee that the family will not have to endure a painful clash with the undertaker in making such arrangements."

Of course not all who urge funeral reform are dedicated to the memorial service. Groups have been formed for various reasons: to take care of death needs at lower cost (often under labor union sponsorship); to offer a simpler rite than traditional church funerals do; or to bypass what some term the "brutal" negotiations between the mortician and the bereaved individual. About 120 societies are members of the Continental Association of Funeral and Memorial Societies, Inc. Others with union affiliations remain independent, some once affiliated with Continental are now independent, and still other groups use the name but are funeral-director sponsored, in response to the threat of the competition. Most legitimate funeral reform or memorial societies are nonprofit and membership-controlled.

The societies are largely deprecated, if not openly opposed, by the funeral industry, even though societies affiliated with Continental work through existing mortuaries, by contract or unwritten agreement, to furnish mortuary services to society members. The societies are not licensed funeral establishments themselves, and the members are required to use the mortuaries named by the society.

One opponent of the memorial service idea, Dr. George E. LaMore, Jr., believes the practice is lacking in respect and reverence:

> Minimum confrontation with death, minimum ministry and ceremony for the living through funeralization and minimum cost conspire to deal with the deceased after the matter of Dixie Cups and facial tissue in our throw-away culture. They are simply disposable, and sheer matter of economy is raised as justification enough. There is a terrible cheapening of both life and death implied by all this, especially when seen in the context of the larger liturgies of respect and reverence practiced in human cultures the world round. . . .

Ernest Morgan, humanist counsellor at the Arthur Morgan School and leading spokesman for the memorial society movement, denies this:

> If some of us at time of death wish to have the remains of our loved ones taken promptly and quietly for simple burial, or for cremation without casket, embalming or ceremony, it is not because we are stingy or because we are lacking in sentiment. On the contrary, it is because we wish our memory image of the departed to be centered on a life in its fullness, and not on a corpse—no matter how skillfully prepared.

Morgan plays down the heavy stress on the memorial service rite and against viewing, and suggests that the memorial society movement emphasize preplanning of all funeral or memorial rites, no matter what kind an individual wants. In his book, *A Manual of Death Education* (Burnsville, N.C.: Celo Press, 1975), he indicates the movement's strong identification with anti-funeral sentiment has alienated the less affluent and poorly educated by deprecating their desires for more elaborate funeral rites and expenditures than present members feel fitting. "In practice, this may mean, for one thing, that members not be required to accept the concept of simplicity, but be helped to get the kind of services they want at costs they can afford."

But this permissiveness is not apparent in the denunciations of the American funeral by others from among memorial society ranks. One author writes that the funeral, "with all its vulgarity, sacrifice of spiritual values to materialist trappings, immature indulgence in privative spectacles, unethical business practices, and overwhelming abnegation of rational attitudes—has become for many students of the national scene a symbol of cultural sickness."

While as preplanning groups the memorial societies may have a broad-base appeal in America at some future time, to date the American preference in funerary service remains tied to the commercial funeral tradition, even though new variations throughout the country indicate changing religious and sociological values. Although data vary, even those who wish it were not so agree that 90 percent, if not more, of Americans continue to bury their dead, hold religious funerals, and engage in open-casket viewing.

An unorganized but vocal anti-funeral sentiment is also heard for the elimination of all ceremonials and rites connected with death. Many of those who support this point of view base it on an antireligious but essentially ethical philosophy that equates any ritualistic ceremony for the dead with a denial of one's social commitment to the living and the wonders of scientific and medical advancement. As these arguments are in line with observed trends in America of substituting secular for religious values and reducing all ritual connected with the funeral, it appears that such a philosophical attitude is on the increase.

In a work entitled *Death, Bereavement and Mourning,* published in 1965, the British anthropologist Geoffrey Gorer focuses on whether or not the elimination of all formal funeral ritual had any long-range effects on members of the population. Dr. Gorer made a study of contemporary English burial and cremation practices, which by and large are already characterized by a minimum of funeral rituals, strong sentiment for cremation, perfunctory (if any) religious rites, and a barely perceptible post-mortem ritualized period of mourning.

His conclusions were that this deritualization is quite deleterious, finding "the lack of accepted ritual and guidance is accompanied by a very considerable amount of maladaptive behavior." Noting that "one possible outcome of the public denial of mourning is a great increase in public callousness," he feels that "the majority of British people are today without adequate guidance . . . and without social help in living through and coming to terms with the grief and mourning which are the inevitable responses in human beings to the death of someone they have loved."

Recent psychiatric literature in America strongly corroborates this point of view. As yet, there seems to have been no documented research to prove the contrary.

4

Costs—and "A Fitting Funeral"

The importance of the cost and the degree of simplicity or ostentation in a funeral obviously fall in the realm of relative values. Still, if your survivors are to be considered, the costs of the funeral certainly must be weighed alongside all the other factors. If money is no object, as was stipulated by the client of a well-known estate attorney in southern California, then his insistence on a $40,000 mausoleum in a private park for his casket and those of his family is his own business. Otherwise mortuary costs must be kept in mind, even if they aren't the sole criterion of choice. The amount you plan to spend on the funeral will either decrease your estate or can lay a heavy savings burden on your survivors now to cover any preburial layaway plans you make.

HOW ARE COSTS COMPUTED?

It's helpful to know what funeral and burial or cremation costs are today and how they are derived in order to see them in relation to other costs. The details may appear tedious at first, but they are necessary in order to put later figures into perspective.

There are four methods morticians use to quote prices, the only difference among them being how the total (which remains the same) is split up.

The traditional method of pricing funeral goods and services is the single-unit method. In this, the funeral director quotes one price to cover a "unit of service" which is called the "standard adult funeral." This figure includes three separate categories. The first is the funeral director's professional services and those of the staff: picking up the body and bringing it to the home; embalming the corpse and working the features into a reasonable likeness of the person; providing consulting services for the survivors; and handling all the organizational details necessary in seeing the funeral and burial is carried out properly, according to the wishes of the next of kin. The second category includes the use of the facilities: the storage room, the preparation room, the viewing room, the chapel, and other areas for receptions or gatherings (including, of course, the parking lot). Finally, there is the cost of the casket. Although the proportionate cost of each of these varies, the elaborateness of the casket usually determines the price of the package. The difference between a $400 funeral and a $900 one often rests on the choice of the casket.

When the single-unit pricing method is used, the price that is usually displayed on top of the casket in the showroom is this "standard adult funeral," the cost of all three items.

The bi-unit method of pricing separates the price of the casket from the other two items; the tri-unit method separates all three items; and a multi-unit method itemizes by function, giving the separate charges for the various pieces of equipment, the use of the motor vehicles, and so forth.

In addition to the basic charges there are the "optionals," although in some cases these are hardly optional at all. These are charged separately, over and above the cost shown on the casket. There is the cost of burial clothing (if the survivor does not furnish this), the honorarium for the clergyman and other religion-related costs, the limousines (unless specifically indicated as part of the price of the funeral), additional motor equipment, flowers, newspaper death notices (which surprisingly must be paid for), and any transportation costs outside a certain radius.

Another thing that the funeral home may charge for, although it is actually a cemetery cost, is an "interment receptacle," that is, the burial vault in which the casket is placed before lowered into the cemetery lot, or a cemetery lot liner, placed directly in the grave, around and above the casket.

Then there are the cemetery costs, which are over and above what must be paid the funeral director. If you choose earth burial these costs include: a cemetery lot and the grave liner (if not purchased from the funeral director); opening and closing grave charges (digging the grave, placing the liner in it, refilling the grave after the casket has been placed in it, and the resodding); endowment fund assessment for perpetual care (if the cemetery is an endowment-fund park); the grave marker or memorial stone (usually purchased from or through the cemetery); and possible installation charges for the stone.

If you choose to be entombed (buried above the ground) then the cost of the mausoleum crypt takes the place of the cost of the lot and grave liner; other charges are analogous. The opening and closing charges include placing the casket into the crypt and the sealing. A memorialization plaque or inscription usually replaces the grave marker.

If the body is to be cremated after the funeral service, the cost of cremation is usually advanced by the funeral home, although the actual cremation is done at a cemetery (however, some states permit mortuaries to own their own crematories). If the remains are to be preserved in a columbarium, additional charges are made for the urn, niche, and inscription on the niche front.

What will the total package come to? Unfortunately there is no general answer to that because, like the list price of automobiles, the large lump-sum quotation (in this case the standard adult funeral single-unit price), which itself varies across the country, is augmented by the extras, which can add appreciably to the unit price.

Many private and governmental studies have been made to show the "average" costs charged by funeral homes. The figures, when specific, pertain to only one locality. In addition, the average costs quoted are rather soft figures since, as is often the case, the lowest quotation is an option not often offered or, if offered, is surprisingly seldom chosen. Also, the date of the collection of the data may make the figures less than precise if published long afterwards, particularly in light of recent rapid inflation that has made obsolete even one- or two-year-old cost figures. Moreover, surprisingly few surveys have been made of cemetery costs and little investigation has been done on grave markers or monuments, although both are an integral part of all funeral/burial costs.

Be that as it may, a number of reports that make a partial comparison of funeral costs possible are available.

According to an article in the *Los Angeles Times* of March 1, 1974, reporting the results of a Federal Trade Commission report on its survey of fifty-six funeral homes in Washington, D.C., the average cost per family for funeral home services in 1973 was $1,137. This included the casket, embalming and dressing the body, the use of the viewing room and the chapel, and the use of a hearse and limousine (in other words, the standard adult funeral). The report also gave an average

$750 charge as covering the cost of the cemetery plot and charges, and the gravestone. The total average cost per family to bury one person in the District of Columbia, not counting the funeral home "extras," was $1,887.

Comparable nationwide industry figures were almost the same, according to a *Los Angeles Times* article of June 7, 1975. The National Funeral Directors Association figures showed the average cost per funeral in 1973 to be $1,117. The NFDA also put the additional funeral home and cemetery charges at an average of $750. The NFDA total was $1,867 as compared to that of the FTC Washington, D.C., study of $1,887.

Other industry figures for the nation were higher than the FTC survey. According to an article in the *Chicago Sun-Times* of May 18, 1975, the Federated Funeral Directors of America published a report giving the average price per funeral in 1974 as $1,777. Although the report came out a year later, the figure included more items. In addition to the standard adult funeral, it included such optionals and advances as the burial vault, special clothing, death notice publication, and special music requests. Subtracting the extras, the cost of the base price, comparable to the $1,137 of the FTC study, was $1,287. According to the Funeral Directors Services Association of Greater Chicago the cost in the Chicago area for this package was about $135 more or $1422.

The Maryland Center for Public Broadcasting, a private nonprofit group, published figures in a consumer-oriented pamphlet on funerals for what they called a "typical" funeral, based on either 1973 or 1974 prices in the Baltimore–Washington, D.C. area. Their estimate gave the cost for the standard funeral home package plus extras as $1,600, plus $645 for the grave liner, opening and closing charges, grave marker, and what appears to be the cemetery lot, giving a grand total of $2,245 as the price a family would pay for a funeral and burial.

But the range within each category of options is enormous. According to still another article from *Better Homes and Gardens* as reprinted in the Maryland Center pamphlet, cemetery plots can range from just under $100 to "thousands"; the cost of the motor vehicle to the cemetery from $25 to $85; obituary notices from $6 in a small-town paper to $30 or more in a large metropolitan daily; the funeral services, exclusive of cemetery expenses, ranging from $300 to $1,500; and the cost of the casket varying from about $450 to $2,000 or more. The same article indicated that the cost of cremation starts at $75, but it goes up from there, and the cost of a cremation urn runs from a little under $100 to hundreds of dollars.

If one wants to be entombed, the cost is ordinarily considerably more than being buried, but not if the entombment is in Nashville, Tennessee, according to an article in the *Los Angeles Times* of April 8, 1973. In a twenty-story high-rise mausoleum there, one can get crypt burial, including casket and embalming, according to an official of the corporation, for $1,895 to $2,900 (exempting the most expensive crypt costing $350 more). This approximates the $2,245 cost quoted by the Maryland Center—but there were no specifics of whether "extras" would inflate the figure.

Regional differences in all categories are noticeable. According to a brochure put out by Los Angeles public television station KCET, 1974 figures gathered in the area appear both lower and higher than the *Better Homes and Gardens* article. The range of caskets was from "a few hundred dollars" to $6,000 and up.

Where competition operates, prices tend to be similar, although the percentage differences of the small money amounts tend to be high. The cost of cremation in southern California indicates that the difference in the prices charged by the "for profit" organizations as compared to the nonprofit memorial societies was not large, but it amounts to about a fifteen percent differential in cost.

According to the brochure of one such for-profit organization, it costs the amount of the social security lump-sum death benefit ($255) to pick up a body, cremate it immediately, and scatter the remains in the ocean (with no mortuary involved). The only additional cost is a $15 registration fee for an individual, or $25 for a couple, payable either by the donor before death or the survivor after the death takes place.

Another for-profit organization charges $250 to pick up the body, cremate it immediately, and scatter the ashes in the ocean (no mortician involved), plus a before-need membership fee of $15 per person or $25 per couple. However, for the same service it charges nonmembers (presumably after death takes place) $50 more, or $300.

In contrast one nonprofit funeral society in the area has an immediate cremation, scattering of ashes plan (one of many plans they offer, handled by a licensed mortician) that costs $234.50, plus a before-death membership fee of $5 per individual or $10 per family. Similarly another memorial society in the area charges $215 for the same service and membership fee.

Regional figures, unfortunately, can be deceptive, particularly in a place like southern California, an industry spokesman says, where prices are "more competitive than elsewhere." Even at that, it might be useful to see what one particular funeral and burial cost in the Los Angeles area in 1973. The mortuary services and interment took place at one of the large mortuary/cemetery combination corporations peculiar to California although found in other states throughout the nation.

In this case the cemetery lot was purchased by the couple several years before the woman suddenly died, but none of the other funeral home services had been arranged beforehand. However, when the lot had been purchased through a salesman who visited the couple, they were asked how much they thought of spending on a funeral. They said: "About $1,000."

The bi-unit priced statement that eventually came to the widower after the death was itemized as follows:

1. Mortuary services and facilities	$	415.00
2. Casket		97.00
3. Newspaper notices		15.00
4. Flowers		35.00
5. Cash advanced: clergyman, $35; coroner's fee (because it was a sudden death), $50		85.00
6. Burial plot (total)		300.00
7. Opening and closing charges		114.00
8. Permit and filing fees		25.00
9. Concrete vault		122.00
10. Memorial tablet (including installation)		163.80
11. Vase for flowers (on gravesite)		12.50
12. Endowment Care Fund deposit		20.00
Total (with state and city taxes)		$1,428.36

Obviously these figures are not typical, since those from Washington, D.C., Chicago, and the national average put the entire package closer to $2,000 than $1,000. But as previously mentioned, costs are lower in southern California.

And in another respect, the figures are very representative. In a later chapter in Part III, it will be shown that a survivor must think in terms of allowing an additional one-half the cost of the standard funeral in estimating the cost of the total funeral/burial package. In this case, a $1,000 funeral ended up costing $1,428 for everything, which is just under the $1,500 of the projected cost.

THE FITTING FUNERAL

But even a $2,000 price tag must be put into perspective. The question remains: What is a fitting funeral, a proper funeral at which not too much money is spent and yet one that seems right in terms of the person who died, the family and the community of friends and acquaintances?

This goes back to value judgments again. It is in the light of what is fitting that opponents of the American funeral are most incensed, finding instances of extravagant trappings and unseemly expenditures the antithesis of proper dignity, simplicity, and economy.

Yet obviously "simple" and "dignified" as well as "elaborate" and "expensive" are in the eye of the beholder. One large ethnic group in America, the Chinese, has always regarded a huge expenditure on the casket and the funeral as a cultural imperative, whether the funeral is Christian or Buddhist, often regardless of whether or not the survivor arranging the funeral is American-born. It is not unusual for a family to spend $3,000 for a bronze casket and $10,000 for the processional and burial—and many funerals are far more costly than that. One writer who described such a Chinese funeral with dismay saw persons who indulged in such extravagance as "ideal victims for exploiters—prizes eagerly sought by merchants of mortality." Yet one wonders in this case how the immediate cremation of the body followed by a memorial service, at a cost of $250, would be a more "dignified" solution.

Standards of dignity, economy, and fitness have meaning

only in each particular instance. The standards vary with age, ethnic background, religious upbringing or religious disassociation, social standing, public noteworthiness, economic status, concern for or indifference to community norms, and so on. According to a study done some ten years ago by sociologists V. R. Pine and D. L. Phillips, even among people with less sharply defined cultural patterns than the Chinese, and among all economic backgrounds (though less so among the wealthy), survivors regarded the amount of money spent and the elegance of the funeral as a reflection not only of what the community felt but what *they* felt showed their respect and esteem for the one who died. There seems evidence that this is more true now than it was then.

As one who is prearranging one's own funeral, you may think the same, taking into consideration your position in the community, the people who would come to your funeral and burial, and the status of the survivors whom you leave behind.

In terms of cost, what does a $2,000 commitment of non-utilitarian expenditure mean to you and your family? For a low-income wage earner earning $8,000 a year, this amount represents three months' wages. For a moderately successful corporate attorney, this may be a little over a week's salary and hardly even to be commented upon.

There is no absolute answer. This is a personal decision you (that is, you alone, or both of you, or all of you) must make.

5

Arranging the Funeral and Burial

As soon as you've made your decision, make the arrangements to put the decision into operation: Choose the mortuary to take care of your funeral and buy a burial plot for your body (or crypt space or a niche in a columbarium).

How firm these arrangements are to be depends, of course, on your age and how settled you are in the community. If you are not yet living in the area where you intend to settle for a while (if not indefinitely), then hold off buying a cemetery lot. That piece of real estate may be unusable if you should leave the city; you will continue to own it, but only for burial purposes.

Your living situation may be so fluid that it may not even be wise to choose a mortuary at this time. In this case, simply sit down and write a "Letter of Instructions on Funeral and Burial" to your spouse, next of kin, or "to whom it may concern." In it, put down specific instructions about your funeral and burial which *any* mortuary can fill. File it with your papers where it can be found quickly when needed.

The letter should contain the following: what kind of disposition (burial, cremation, or donation to a medical school). If the last, indicate if you've signed a Uniform Donor Card, the institution you prefer, if you've made any arrangements, and any other information relating to the gift. If burial, what kind (earth or entombment) and preference of location or situation if any. If cremation, what is to be done with the ashes. What kind of service (memorial, funeral, or none), where should it be held (home, church, funeral home, or elsewhere); public or private. Church denomination, if any; clergyman or another to preside; hymns, music, soloist if any; other religious arrangements. Should there be flowers? Any wishes in lieu of flowers? Do you have an expense limit? Include a short biography from which information can be extracted for the obituary. Add anything else you feel pertinent.

Write your funeral and burial instructions as though they'll go into effect within a year, but try to keep them as flexible as possible to give your next of kin leeway in making arrangements.

Another solution to a fluid living situation is to join a memorial society. The advantage to this is that if you belong to a society that is a member of the Continental Association, in general there is a reciprocal membership among the groups. There may be a problem if you move. Usually you can transfer your membership and mortuary instructions to the group in the new city (if there is such a group there). Note, however, that this transfer is not automatic. The many societies differ in their membership fees, the alternative plans they offer, and the conditions of membership. So you cannot rely exclusively on this being a total solution to your problem.

SELECTING A MORTUARY

If you are fairly settled in your community, look for a mortuary to take care of your funeral and burial needs.

If you've become a member of a funeral society or memorial society, your choice of mortuary is limited to those working with the society. To find out which these are, write for a membership application to the local society chapter. (If you don't know the name and can't find it in the phone book, write to the Continental Association of Funeral and Memorial Societies, Washington, D.C., for the nearest one.) When you return the membership fee to the local group, they will send you a list of cooperating mortuaries, together with the optional plans available and a price list of all the services the mortuaries offer. There may be a number of cooperating mortuaries, so you will have to choose one from the group.

On the open market you have greater choices. If you confine your choice to a mortuary that serves your particular religious faith or, even more specifically, your particular church, you are limiting your options, but depending on your religion you still have a number to choose from. Funeral homes that specialize in Christian funerals hold both Protestant and Catholic funerals; in a large city this number is quite large. Catholic funeral homes, even when they cater predominantly to a Catholic clientele, usually will conduct Protestant services if asked. Nonsectarian homes hold funerals for all faiths, or for those of no religious persuasion at all.

Jewish mortuaries conduct only Jewish funerals; and Jews traditionally go only to known Jewish funeral homes if there are any such in the community. This exclusivity may be rather constricting. In Chicago, for example, a quarter of a million people are served by only three exclusively Jewish funeral firms. However this situation often can be alleviated since there are no doctrinal reasons for this preference but only customary practice. A startling example of this occurred recently in a Midwestern city when a group of Orthodox Jews who wanted to arrange simple funerals at a fixed price could get no cooperation from any of the Jewish mortuaries. They simply took their patronage to a group of non-Jewish funeral homes who were happy to work out a satisfactory arrangement with them.

A similar situation exists in the black community. Here too, tradition, preference, and community cohesiveness work together to keep black mortuaries catering to a black clientele. Those who wish to exercise options elsewhere have all the Christian and nonsectarian mortuaries to choose from. The Black Muslims, however, limit their choice to mortuaries run or sanctioned by their church.

If no reason points you toward one establishment rather than another, then you have the widest choice of all to shop around to find the kind of mortuary that you want. And shop around you must, since various independent consumer and government groups have found that both prices and services vary widely in the same area.

Reliability and compatibility are two qualities you'll want to look for besides price, since one of the reasons for making preneed arrangements is so that your spouse or next of kin can get the right reassurance and support from the funeral director when you die. You don't want the director subtly to resist your expressed wishes, or pressure your spouse into spending more than you all agreed was sufficient, or, worst of all, engage in any fraudulent or unethical behavior when you are not around to object.

Compatibility is particularly important if you're interested in a nonconventional service. Make sure you find a congenial mortician if you have strong ideas on nonviewing of the body, or certain convictions about children at the funeral home, or the presence or absence of flowers, or the use of tape recorders or cameras, or the presence of the news media (if you are a newsworthy person). Of course the same holds true if you are a traditionalist and want to be certain that all the conventional customs and rituals are followed.

Go with your spouse if you can, or with a friend—or go alone. Let the mortician tell you what can be offered, then ask about the combination of options you want. Despite popular mythology to the contrary, morticians come in all human shapes, with varying degrees of highmindedness and understanding—with the curve skewing in the ethical direction, according to psychologist Robert Kavanaugh, former Catholic priest and present teacher and consultant on thanatology. On the basis of his experience, Dr. Kavanaugh feels that the fear that a mortician will not render any of the less traditional options (no embalming, no casket if cremation is desired, no viewing of the remains) just isn't true. "The truth is," he writes, "enlightened professional funeral directors will permit almost any combination of options, willing to gain and maintain community respect and regard even while maybe losing money." With a little effort you can find the mortician who will offer the arrangements you want, at what you both feel is a fair price.

In any case, ask hard questions about the "extra" charges if price is a real consideration. Have the mortician show you around the facilities. Later check out the establishment's reputation for reliability and understanding.

After you decide on a mortuary, go there and come to a firm agreement on options and price. Then put all your wishes down in writing on a form the funeral director will give you. Don't hesitate to do this. This "memorial record" does not obligate you in any way, but it certainly will save your spouse or survivors much grief later on.

You will want to list your church affiliation, if any, and the name of the clergyman you prefer to conduct the service, if any. (If you wish, the funeral director will arrange for a clergyman if you have no individual whom you prefer.) If you belong to a lodge or fraternal organization that has a special ritual or memorial service, the funeral home must know the name of the organization and the name of the person or committee to notify. If a veteran, do you want to take advantage of the free flag for draping on your casket, then given to your spouse? The funeral director arranges for this. Specify the type of casket you want, the music you'd like played, any particular passage from the Bible or other literature to be read, the flowers and the colors preferred, even facts for the obituary. These are just some of the details you'll be asked to furnish. (This information is similar to what would be in a "Letter of Instruction.")

You may also want to give the funeral director additional information at this time, information needed to make out the death certificate. This includes vital statistics about your parents, your birthday and citizenship, your social security number, etc. The mortician probably will want a list of immediate family members and close friends to be notified.

The director will also ask if you own a cemetery plot, and if so, where. There may be a family plot in another city. If you may feel you would like to have your body shipped to that city, he must also know the name of a mortuary to whom to ship the body. (If you don't have the name of one, check in his book listing all the mortuaries in the United States.)

If you have a long-standing wish to be buried in a family plot in a country other than the United States, you may also mention this to the mortician. (When death takes place he must make the rather complicated arrangements, which may be costly.)

If you want to be buried in a veterans' cemetery (where the

lots are free to veterans and their closest next of kin) the funeral director will check out the closest one. However the
burial space cannot be reserved; whether you can actually be
buried there later depends on whether the cemetery is still
open for burials when you die.

These detailed instructions do not obligate your survivors
to this particular mortuary (although if you make any monetary arrangements, which are unnecessary at this time, there
may be complications). This list is not a contract in any way.
Should you decide to make arrangements with another mortician for any reason, a simple letter to the first telling him to
cancel the arrangements is all that's necessary.

If possible, make your wishes flexible. Conditions and circumstances change. In any case, make sure your survivors
know what you want and agree to follow through with your
instructions.

There is one other contingency you must consider. Talk it
over with your spouse or companion, later with your attorney—and also your mortician. If you should die on vacation
or on a business trip in this country, the body can be returned
by train or air freight. Unlike older train rules, Amtrak and
airline regulations no longer require anyone to pick up the
body and accompany it back home. But arrangements must
be made with a mortician where the death took place to have
the body embalmed. This is done from home by your survivor; your present mortician arranges to have the far-city
mortician reimbursed later. Clear it with your own mortician
and let your spouse know you've done so. However, if you
plan to be cremated, you may wish to have your remains
returned or have them scattered in the place where you die.

Naming the mortuary of your choice is an important
backup for another reason. If you should die in another country while on vacation or on a business trip, and your next of
kin wishes to have the body returned, the consular officer in

the U.S. embassy or consulate abroad who is contacted and who makes the arrangements must have the name of a mortuary in the home city to which to ship the body. Since there will be little time for your survivors to investigate and decide upon a mortuary, particularly under the shock of the unexpected death and especially if that person is himself or herself overseas, it's best to make sure your survivors have the name of the mortuary on hand just in case.

Once you've completed the funeral arrangements, tell *all* your relatives what you have decided—not only your spouse, but your parents, your sisters and brothers, and your friends. This is to protect the one who must carry out your wishes, particularly if the wishes are out of the ordinary or contrary to what others might do. If you are living with a friend who is not related by law, this is particularly important. Even if your relatives agree to let him or her be responsible, they may change their minds when you die. By making your wishes common knowledge, disgruntled relatives may be deterred from trying to override your explicit preferences.

If you wish your friend, rather than kin, to take charge of your funeral and burial arrangements, you may wish to put the name of this person in your will, together with your specific wishes regarding the disposition of the body. By law, your closest next of kin owns the human remains after your death. However, changing mores are giving rise to a new body of case law and may eventually change the heretofore recognized legal primacy of next of kin in disposing of the body. Putting your preference of the responsible party in your will may give your wishes greater legal stature, although the validity of this stance has yet to be clearly established in the courts of the land.

Carry the mortuary card in your wallet or purse, where the police can find it in case you're accidentally killed. Give your spouse, friend, or older children the name and phone number of the mortuary where all these detailed instructions are on file. Should you have to enter a hospital or nursing home for what may be mortal illness, the hospital should also be given the name of the mortuary for their records.

CHOOSING A CEMETERY

If you feel you don't want to make cemetery arrangements just yet, don't. Just keep in mind that your survivors will have to pay a higher price for a burial plot if it's needed quickly. On the other hand, if you're convinced you're in the community where you intend to live and die (barring unforeseen circumstances) the sooner you see to burial arrangements the better.

Buying a cemetery lot must be done with a bit more care than choosing a mortician. Except for the casket, the mortician is offering you professional services that are personal and subject to personal judgment. Moreover mortuary goods and services aren't actually purchased until you die. But cemeteries deal in real estate, and any transaction you make goes into effect as soon as you sign the contract for the deed. So a different set of standards must apply.

The initial choice of place depends, again, on whether you're limited to a cemetery devoted exclusively to members of your religious faith. Jewish and Catholic cemeteries tend to be exclusive. But there's been a sharp decline in the United States of churches with churchyards restricted to church members and their families alone. Today large cemeteries often are made up of various sections, each devoted to a particular faith or sect, with large nonsectarian areas.

If your family or friends are all buried in one particular cemetery, you may have a strong preference for that particular one, no matter how expensive the lots. But if your options are more flexible, ask your mortician to suggest possible choices. He certainly will know approximate prices at all the cemeteries in the area and the sections where gravesite space is still available. He can give you a good idea of what to look for and how to make the best arrangements, even if he has no specific suggestions or recommendations. Independent mortuaries seldom have any direct connection with a cemetery. It's illegal for a mortuary to be paid by a cemetery to steer business to them.

Consider the mortician's suggestions, perhaps check with your clergyman, then check out the places in person.

When you look over cemetery lots, you will want to weigh price, of course. But there are other things to be considered as well, such as accessibility to your home and the mortuary and the ease with which friends and family can visit the gravesite. Look over the site through their eyes. Check the state of development of the cemetery land. If this is a newly formed cemetery or an undeveloped area of an established one, lots can usually be purchased at a lower price than in a well-built-up area. But make sure the newly formed corporation is viable and legitimate; you want your lot to be available when you die. One memorial park official strongly suggests carefully checking out the reputation of such a cemetery and its board of directors among community and religious leaders. You must also decide (on not many facts) if the lot will still be desirable when you die, particularly if you are looking for a family lot.

If you buy into a new section of an already established cemetery, make certain another lot can be purchased in the developed section if you should die before the new area is open.

Look to how the graves are maintained. Some cemeteries have endowment-care trusts for maintaining the grounds "in perpetuity," paid out of the cost of the lot or separately when buying the lots (with a state agency usually supervising the trust's integrity). Other cemeteries without such trusts make separate arrangements to maintain the grave. Make sure you know how this is done.

As you weigh these tangibles, you must also be weighing the intangibles, hinging on your own perception of the meaning of the cemetery space itself. There's a permanency, a stability feature about a cemetery lot that brings in a number of value judgments. Try to project into the future to see what this piece of land will mean to your spouse after you die, and to your children and grandchildren after she or he dies. Should you think in terms of a family lot? Will you be living around this area long enough to make this grave a real memorial? Will family members remain in the area in large enough numbers to make a group of graves together a meaningful expenditure?

The question of a double lot for you and your spouse, while not quite so symbolic a gesture, still bears serious thought. If you both are getting older, have lived in this area all your lives with no intention of leaving, and it appears unlikely that either of you will remarry if the other should die, then by all means consider buying a double lot. Or consider double interment for the two of you: two caskets in the same space, one above the other. (Such an arrangement, it must be remembered, must be made before the first body is buried.) But if one should die and the other remarry or move to where the children live or to a retirement community far away, the second half of the double lot will remain unused, so much idle real estate with little resale value. (Cemeteries are notoriously reluctant to buy back lots that cannot be used, although some permit you to resell the deed to another person. The seller usually must go through a cemetery broker, selling off the lot at a highly discounted price, if at all, compared to what the broker gets when the lot is resold to someone else.)

If you are checking on lot prices, make sure you also check out the cemetery opening and closing costs, the need for and the cost of a grave liner, and all the unlisted but inevitable additional costs that make up the total package, *including* the charges for the endowment fund. Be sure you ask about the marker or gravestone. Check if you can purchase a gravestone elsewhere–and if so, if there are special cemetery charges to install the stone on the plot.

At this point you may even want to go to the monument dealer and talk about the gravestone. You are not looking to buy anything just yet. But it's helpful for you and your survivors to know these facts:

Monuments and markers were once made of many materials; now granite and bronze plaques are the most common (bronze being the less expensive). Marble, slate, or sandstone, once used exclusively, weather so badly that they are now rarely if ever used.

Granite comes in all colors: black, gray, soft reds, white. The finest stones have an absence of any discoloration or seams, with a fine, uniform grain texture and color throughout.

The size of the stone, the number of words in the inscription, and any special borders or designs all affect the price. All stones are handcrafted, so prices can range from $400 and up for flat, flush-to-the-ground markers, and $600 and up for the upright stone, not including installation. As one expert in the business writes, "it is that 'and up' that really counts. Large, complex memorials can cost several thousand dollars." But this is more than a lifetime investment, he maintains. It's one that will remain as long as there is anyone around to see the grave itself.

As soon as you've made up your mind about the cemetery
—and a number of days or weeks may intervene while you
evaluate the choices and talk it over with others—return to
the cemetery you've decided on and conclude the agreement.

6

Paying the Funeral and Cemetery Costs

After you've arranged all the details of your funeral and burial, you must decide how and when to pay for them: now, later, or not at all.

AVAILABLE DEATH BENEFITS FUNDS

Today there are a number of government sources that will provide your survivors with some of the money. In addition, there may be private sources that you already have which will furnish more.

SOCIAL SECURITY LUMP-SUM DEATH BENEFIT

If you are insured under social security, your spouse or whoever takes responsibility to pay for your funeral and burial gets $255 when you die. For those who aren't eligible for social security (United States military personnel, federal civil servants, some state and local government employees, and those covered under the Railroad Retirement Act), an equivalent sum is usually (not always) available.

VETERANS ADMINISTRATION FUNERAL AND BURIAL ALLOWANCE

The VA has a benefit for the survivor of a veteran who has not been dishonorably discharged: $250 for funeral costs, $150 for the cost of a cemetery lot (if the body isn't buried in a national cemetery, where burial is free), and a free burial marker. This sum may also be claimed by whoever takes responsibility for the funeral or burial.

FRATERNAL SOCIETY, ETHNIC GROUP, UNION BENEFITS

You may be a member of a lodge, fraternal group, or union that provides a lump-sum death benefit to pay funeral costs. Many groups have such "burial benefits" as one of their membership fringe benefits. The money can range from as low as $100 to amounts covering the total costs, as in the case of many unions. If you don't know whether any apply to you, check these out now to make sure. Then let whomever may be taking the responsibility know how much you have, and with what organization.

As for the rest of the money, you must decide whether your survivors need any additional special funds, and if so, how you can make special provision now to cover them.

The advantage of taking care of the funeral and burial costs now is that by doing so, you'll remove one immediate and very traumatic decision from your survivors' repertoire of worries when you die.

The disadvantage of doing so now is that the event may not take place for some time. In the interim, circumstances change—and the money you so carefully put aside now may or may not be available to, or *remembered* by, your survivors when they are faced with the problem of paying for the funeral.

To help your survivors and yet keep all options open as much as possible, you have a number of alternatives, three of which have more built-in flexibility than others.

FUNERAL COSTS PREPAYMENT

If you wish, you may choose not to do anything at all about prepaying your funeral expenses. Let the money come out of your estate's assets when you die. If it's obvious that there will be money in your estate as insurance, savings, or cashable stocks or bonds, this is all the protection your survivor needs. The money you ordinarily would tie up for funeral payments now can be invested or put into savings instead.

The disadvantage of this course is that your estate may never be so large as to cover the funeral costs adequately. Another possibility is that even if you are well off now, your financial fortunes may change, expenses and debts may mount, and your estate may shrink to such a degree that there won't be much money in the estate when you die. In such cases, your survivors would be under great financial strain to meet the cost of your funeral and burial, perhaps going into insurance money or other resources more urgently needed to live on.

To hedge against this possibility, you have a number of choices.

PERSONAL SAVINGS ACCOUNT

One way to cover after-death expenses is by setting up a savings account to cover your funeral and burial needs. Start a regular savings account in a bank or credit union to which you add regularly, allowing the interest to accumulate (or withdrawing it as you please). Some banks permit these accounts to be earmarked as funeral accounts. In most, however, it is simply a regular savings account privately earmarked for after-death expenses.

Its advantage is that it is an unencumbered account. The money is available during your lifetime for unexpected emergencies, and the money can be used for nonfuneral expenses by your survivor if it turns out there is money coming from other sources to cover the death expenses.

The advantage for some people becomes a disadvantage for others. Because it is simply a regular savings account, too often people who are chronically short of money dip into the account regularly instead of keeping it inviolate. Then when death occurs, the money that should have accumulated to take care of the funeral expenses simply is not there.

SMALL, RENEWABLE TERM INSURANCE

This is another device that can be used—a regular insurance policy that is purchased for a specific period of time (five- or ten-year term) for a flat premium. At the end of the term, it can be renewed for another term, but at a higher premium. (Term insurance is explained in more detail in another chapter.)

Its advantage is that it is regular insurance. It comes payable to your spouse or whoever is the beneficiary when you die, therefore it's not limited to where you live or tied in with any particular mortuary or burial plan. Another advantage is that it's relatively inexpensive.

Its major disadvantage for many people is that, like all term insurance, it is never "paid up." It is insurance, pure and simple; while it is in effect, you are insured for its full face value for a small premium. But if the premiums are not paid up, or if the insurance is not renewed when the term expires, the insurance lapses and the coverage disappears.

ARRANGEMENTS LINKED WITH A SPECIFIC FUNERAL HOME

When you make your funeral arrangements, the mortician may suggest that you also arrange to pay the difference, over and above social security and VA benefits, in one of a number of alternative ways. Even when there is no question whether the money is safe or not (and this will be discussed subsequently), there are a number of reasons why you should think this through carefully before committing yourself. In general it has serious drawbacks.

Many things can happen in the intervening years between making initial arrangements with this specific mortuary and your eventual death. You may move out of the area, your next of kin may forget about your arrangements (or not even know about them in the first place), the records with the funeral home's name on it can be lost, or the mortuary itself may go out of business in the five, fifteen, or fifty years from now until then. As a result your next of kin will end up paying for a funeral at another mortuary, not knowing that the funeral has already been prepaid.

In addition, if you change your mind about using this funeral home or move from the area you'll have to get the money back. While legally it's yours, since they can't claim the money until the goods and services are delivered, to do so may involve much effort and negotiation, possibly even threat of legal action (although one hopes not). If your survivors try to recover, there may be even greater difficulty. And not all the money may be recovered even then. Some states permit a funeral home to withhold administrative expenses, which may be as high as twenty-five percent of the money paid in, before returning the remaining funds to the depositor or a survivor.

However, for those who are elderly or who are rooted in one place and have no intention of moving, it is a relatively painless way of paying what will have to be paid eventually. Some people also know their own habits of procrastination well enough to realize that unless they nail down the money now, their survivors will surely have to pay the price.

There are a number of arrangements that can be made, some quite good, some much more shaky.

Time-Payment Contract, Money Not Held in Trust. This is a contract between you and the mortician in which you agree to pay regular installments toward the cost of a prearranged funeral (and burial), with built-in carrying charges, until the total agreed-upon amount is paid up. Then when death occurs the funeral director furnishes the goods and services agreed upon.

Notorious abuses of these contracts have been recorded in the past to such an extent that now thirty-five states forbid them, insisting instead that the funeral homes set up state-supervised trust arrangements for safeguarding the money paid in. Other states have assigned various agencies to watch over these contracts to insure that the principal is safe, the interest charge is not exorbitant, and that the goods and services are indeed provided as stipulated in the contract. But in many states these contracts are still largely unsupervised, and abuses regularly surface.

For example, the fine print of some contracts stipulates that if the purchaser dies before the entire contract is paid off, the balance becomes immediately payable in full and the participating funeral home is under no obligation to perform any service until full payment is made by the survivor. In other contracts the seller has the right to declare the contract null and void if the buyer falls more than thirty days behind in paying any installments, and the seller keeps all previous payments. In still others, from 25 to 30 percent of the total contract price is used to absorb sales and administrative costs. In one type of joint savings account made with a funeral home, the one who makes the prearrangement actually agrees to a loan by a loan company for the stipulated amount, which is put into the account. It is then necessary to pay off the loan, plus interest, plus credit insurance to cover the balance in regular monthly installments; until this is done the funeral director keeps the passbook.

To guard against these and other abuses the National Funeral Directors Association suggests that you make certain that any prepaid agreement you sign provides that all money paid in advance, including the burial vault, be put in trust or in a protected savings account with *you* maintaining control of the account; that you be entitled to all the interest earned, to withdraw or apply to the principal as you choose; and that you retain the right to terminate the contract at any time without forfeiture of any funds paid in or the interest accrued.

Two arrangements now widely used that give protection to funds paid in advance are the joint savings account and the trust fund account.

Funeral Savings Account. The jointly held passbook savings account, taken out by you and the funeral director, is a device usually used by smaller funeral homes that find trust accounts hard to maintain. These accounts are open-ended only in one direction, toward you. You put money into it just as in any savings account, either in regular installments or at irregular intervals, and you may withdraw the money or the interest as you wish. The funeral director, who is named beneficiary of that account, cannot touch the money until your death. At that time the money accumulated is withdrawn to cover the cost of the previously arranged funeral.

The disadvantage of this method is that your survivors are committed to a particular funeral director, with all the disadvantages of a locked-in arrangement mentioned before.

Funeral Trust Fund. The trust unfortunately has the same disadvantage. In this arrangement the funeral home opens up a trust account in your name at a bank, and the money paid in is put into interest-bearing debentures or placed in restricted nonspeculative investments. This trust is supervised by a state agency. The interest from the bonds or investments, which is not very large, can be withdrawn if you wish, although some funeral homes will try to get you to allow the interest to remain in the fund to protect them against inflation.

One drawback with this scheme, a practical rather than a theoretical one, is poor supervision. It sometimes may be serious. Unless the trusts are properly supervised to make sure the investments are sound and the funeral home itself is working through a proper bank, the trust may be no safer than the funeral home itself, which in some cases can be questionable.

Funeral Insurance. The purchase of life insurance of a small face value (from $500 to $2000) to cover funeral and burial costs is still very common—7½ million new policies were sold in 1970. Called "industrial insurance," the yearly premiums are met by paying small weekly or monthly installments, with carrying charges built into the cost.

Its main advantage is that it is a means whereby poor people can cover their funeral and burial costs in increments they can afford—although in the long run the premium costs are high and last a long period of time. (According to Consumers Union, the yearly premium paid this way is at a rate 20 to 25 percent greater than when paid once a year on a larger policy.)

Even more to its detriment, this insurance is sometimes unregulated when the policies are sold across state lines, thus escaping the surveillance of state insurance regulatory agencies. Today, even though federal as well as state credit protection mechanisms exist to guard the consumer, abuses regularly come to light.

One type of special-purpose insurance now written by a number of large insurance companies is known specifically as "funeral insurance." This is a limited, ordinary life policy that is paid up in a relatively short time. When death takes place, the cash face value, also small ($500 to $5000), is paid off to the beneficiary. This insurance, however, often has a tie-in with a specific funeral home; as such, it has all the built-in disadvantages of such an arrangement.

When you buy this insurance, the agents ask you to sign a release authorizing a specific funeral home to receive the money to cover the cost of your funeral or to attach a separate order instructing your beneficiary as to your choice of mortuary. You are not required to do so, of course. However, if you don't, the insurance salesman often contacts the funeral home who in turn gets in touch with you, requesting to handle your funeral arrangements. (They may add the inducement of permitting smaller payments than the quarterly payments required in the policy, part of a time-payment contract.)

BURIAL COST PREPAYMENT

Payment of burial costs is different from payment of funeral goods and services. Since burial involves a piece of real estate, the manner of payment is akin to property purchase. In most cases, unless the lot is paid for in full, it is purchased on a regular time-payment contract with so much down and with regular monthly payments over a specified period. The carrying charges are as permitted in the state for such contracts, with the default provision of all such contracts. If the payments are not kept up, the cemetery lot is forfeited.

The larger cemeteries or memorial park complexes loan the money on their own, others write the loan but a regular finance company carries it at their permitted interest charges, which are high .Often it's wiser to take out a lower interest loan at a bank or credit union to cover the cost, and pay off the lot in cash.

7

Disposing of Your Worldly Possessions: The Will

Just as surely as we avoid making funeral arrangements, we shun making out our wills. Less than one-fourth of all Americans get around to making one before they die, even though many admit that they should. Drawing up a will seems to be an open admission of our limited mortality. As one man said, "When the will is being prepared, the testator is in effect taking stock of his entire life in a form of a self-imposed confessional."

Yet dying without a will, even for those who feel their estate is very modest indeed, usually ends up causing all kinds of difficulties for the survivors. If it's an estate of any substance, the complications can be tremendous. A very notorious instance of this in recent years has been the much publicized court battles involving the heirs of Pablo Picasso, a man who left an estate of more than one billion dollars—and no will.

But even in ordinary, noncontentious cases, problems will

arise. Many can be reduced, if not eliminated completely, if you take time now to draw up your will.

The will is a document drawn up sometime during your lifetime that declares your intentions of how you want your "estate" (that is, all that you own) distributed when you die. Until you die, it can always be changed, added to, replaced, or destroyed. When you die, it becomes a binding legal instrument that sets the rules regarding the redistribution of your property.

The property will be distributed in any case. The state will decide the manner of distribution if you do not. But dying without a will has so many disadvantages that the main arguments for making out a will are best stated in negative terms.

When you die intestate (without a will) the probate court (or "surrogate court" or "orphans court" or whatever the name in your state) appoints an administrator to supervise the distribution of the property. The administrator appointed often is the closest inheriting next of kin (which may or may not be good for your estate, depending on how complicated its business affairs are and your relationship to that person). This administrator is accorded a commission by the court, a percentage of the total value of the assets. Obviously if the administrator is *not* someone you would have chosen, the amount of the commission is lost to your heirs.

The administrator must post a surety bond that is costly (in some states $10 per $1,000 of the estate assets, renewable annually until the estate is settled). The attorney suggested by the administrator is appointed for the various legal work and is also paid a commission out of your estate. In most states the commission is set by statute, but in some states the size of the commission is established at the discretion of the court, and has been known to run as high as 10 percent of the estate's worth.

Another court-appointed person is the appraiser to evaluate

the property. The appraiser's fee also comes out of the estate, this time as a percentage of the property evaluated. When the evaluated property includes such items as cash and securities the fee can be huge. And if there's property in another state, still another appraiser in *that* state must be appointed—and paid from the estate.

Then there are the children, whose interests the court assumes to be different from and possibly antagonistic to those of your spouse, since their portion of the inheritance is cut away from hers or his. If the children are minors, someone must be appointed to approve your spouse's capability as guardian of the children's property. And even if your spouse *is* appointed guardian, she or he must be bonded (money out of the estate) and must account closely to the court for any action taken that might affect the children's separate inheritances.

Then there's the way the state statute determines who inherits what. The rules are determined by marriage or blood relationship; and how the formula is applied is based on the number of relatives alive when you die, how close their relationship was to you, and whether or not you live in a community property state.

The formula is predetermined and rigid—and while the distribution may be just the way you would have apportioned your estate, the chances are that it won't be. The number of "typical" family situations upon which the intestate laws are based are very few in real life. And once you die, the impersonal process set into motion is unalterable.

Bequests to charity are given no recognition. Persons with whom you're very close, either taking care of you or living with you, get no part of your inheritance if they are not related by blood or law. Neither does your divorced spouse nor her or his children, nor any number of persons with whom you may have a special relationship.

Your business may have to be liquidated, your estate may be subject to federal and state taxes at the highest rate, and your heirs may have to wait an inordinate length of time until your assets are freed to pass to them.

You can see why now is the time to make out your will.

WHO SHOULD HAVE A WILL; WHO SHOULD DRAW UP THE WILL?

According to most practicing attorneys, everyone should make out a will as soon as he or she reaches the age of majority. This blanket injunction includes young, single adults owning what they presume to be negligible property, married women wholly dependent on their husbands' income, older persons with only personal possessions and life insurance—everyone. Almost every textbook and popular treatment on the subject expresses the same sentiment.

Another dictum is this: Have an attorney draw up your will. Corollary: Don't rely on those do-it-yourself books for drawing up a will by yourself. On this latter point, expert legal opinion insists that relying on these books is dangerous and causes more problems than are solved.

Of course attorneys, like doctors, see the botched-up jobs, not the cases that respond well to self-administered remedies. For this reason they may have a more hard-nosed view of possible dire consequences than may actually be the case. And the ones who *write* the do-it-yourself books are also attorneys, presumably as aware of the consequences of an improperly drawn will as those who condemn their efforts.

Still, pursuing the medical analogy further, one can imagine a good case is made by saying that if anything goes wrong when you help yourself to patent medicines to cure what seems like a simple ailment, doctors can later try to correct the damage and save your life. If they can't and you die, at least the consequences were of your own making. But if you die without making a will, or with a badly drawn-up will, no lawyer can reverse the damage after you're dead. The ones who suffer are your heirs, the innocents who were not in any way responsible for your miscalculation. They pay the consequences, not you.

The minimum fee for having a lawyer draw up a simple will is something around $50 to $75 at the time of this writing. For some, this appears excessive—and perhaps it is. For such people free legal aid is often available.

Others who can well afford the $50 and more sometimes insist as a matter of principle they shouldn't have to go to a lawyer for something that is essentially a simple process and, in any case, a personal matter. Among this group are young people who learn for the first time about holographic (hand-written) wills or nuncupative wills (witnessed oral wills made when one is dying).

However, practicing attorneys say these objections are just schoolroom fun-and-games. Even though holographic wills are recognized in twenty-three states and nuncupative wills in forty-two, the circumstances and conditions under which each type is recognized vary greatly from state to state. Often the conditions are so special and circumscribed that the will's validity is always a matter of question, certain to precipitate a court challenge. While there are instances where such wills should be given credence (which is why legislatures have made them legal in the first place), most attorneys, even sympathetic ones with a sense of humor, feel it's hardly worthwhile to avoid having a properly drawn-up will just to test the point, particularly since you won't be around to watch the court battles or suffer any of the consequences.

CHOOSING AN ATTORNEY

If the will is comparatively simple and the estate is not over $20,000, most attorneys can do the job. But if the estate is larger than that amount or it involves rather complicated business and family relationships (even if below that amount), then a specialist should be consulted. If the estate is $250,000 or more, where the tax implications become very important, or the distribution of the estate involves a special or unusual arrangement, then a specialist in wills and estate planning should *certainly* be consulted. Ask your tax accountant, business associates, or, if you have one, your regular lawyer to recommend the name of a large firm with an estate-planning specialist, or a firm that specializes entirely in estate work.

The fee the attorney will charge depends on how complicated the will is and whether there are any trusts or special tax-avoidance provisions. It will also depend on whether or not the attorney is named (or expects to be named) executor or coexecutor of the will. As executor, the attorney will also receive a commission in the probating of the will and will sometimes reduce or even waive a fee for this consideration. If the lawyer doesn't mention it, you should feel perfectly free to do so.

And if your spouse will also be drawing up his or her will at the same time, the charges are often much below double the first fee for both wills, particularly if the second is more or less a mirror image of your own. Both you and your spouse should certainly have separate wills in any case.

It's perfectly proper to inquire about the charge for an attorney's services, including the cost for any phone or interview consultations later. If you feel the fee too high, choose another lawyer.

PRELIMINARIES TO HAVING THE WILL DRAWN UP

After you've decided on an attorney to draw up your will, gather together the material that will be needed to do it properly. If you have it all with you the first time you go to the office, it will save time for both of you (*you* meaning you and the attorney or you as you and your spouse). Otherwise you must make another trip or send the material over subsequently.

Bring along any previous will you may have made. This ordinarily will have to be cancelled, unless the changes are so minor that they can be added as a codicil (amendment) to the earlier version. Actually, if these changes are anything but *very* minor, it's better to write a new one.

For even a simple will, your attorney must have your full name and any others you may have used in your lifetime and the full names and addresses of all beneficiaries. Then you'll have to recount some personal details about your life and your past life that are relevant. In brief, the attorney must know if you've been married before, if your ex-spouse is living, and if there were any children from that marriage; if there are any adopted children or stepchildren in your family; or illegitimate children or undissolved marriages in the past; or relatives in institutions or under special care that must be provided for. You must tell the attorney if your current spouse has been married before and if she or he had children of the earlier marriage; if any of your *children* have any such relationships; if there are any, repeat, *any* complicating blood or in-law relationships that may cause difficulty later.

If the will is more than of the simplest kind, you should have a list with you of all your assets, real and personal. (Real property is land and buildings; personal property is anything that isn't real.) In this inventory should be all that you own. Briefly, have information about your real property, about stocks and bonds, mortgages, bank accounts, life insurance and annuities, valuable personal possessions, and so forth. A lawyer needs this to advise you on setting up the terms of the will to insure that as much of your wealth gets to your beneficiaries as possible. If it looks as though various trust arrangements are in order, more information will be requested and in greater detail.

Have with you a list of specific bequests and gifts you want to make. Bequests can include specific items such as personal property to go to specific people; general bequests, usually sums of money, are often made to charities. Make sure you have the precise names of the charities plus the names of the persons to receive the charitable bequests.

An executor or executrix (a legal term to characterize a female executor) must be named. Who this person should be and whether he or she should serve without bond requires serious thought. You might want to talk it over with your attorney *before* making a decision. But whomever you decide upon, clear it with the person first to make sure he or she agrees to serve. If you don't request clearance, name an alternate in case the first person declines.

The qualifications of the executor or executrix who will administer your will after you die depend on how complicated your affairs are; but if any particular qualifications must be given priority over any others, integrity and a sense of responsibility are most important. If someone with these qualifications doesn't have too much legal or financial expertise (as perhaps your spouse), consider naming the attorney or a bank as coexecutor. Or you may *suggest* that he or she call upon the attorney or a fiduciary agent for assistance, making it a discretionary act rather than a command from you. The duties of the executor will be discussed more fully in Part III.

If the will is comparatively simple, with no ongoing business involved or complicated investments or disputed debts, a survivor with ordinary acumen surely can handle the task without difficulty. Even if it *is* more complicated, a trusted and concerned person with the sense to know when to get expert advice is far better than the efficient but indifferent expert whose concern with other matters makes *your* estate's management a matter of low priority.

WHAT SHOULD THE WILL CONTAIN?

There are a number of standard elements in every will, as your attorney will advise you. First, the will should contain specific language cancelling any previous will. It will give your full name and where you live. It will name your executor or executrix with the attendant conditions and lay out general directions for him or her to follow. It will then give the executor specific instructions on how you want your property disposed of. These will include whatever specific gifts and bequests you want to leave particular people and charities. Also there will be general policy guidelines for the executor, perhaps regarding the children. If you have an ongoing business or property or investments that need discretionary handling, general policy guidelines regarding them will be included. Finally, it designates the person or persons to receive the residue.

Whatever else is found in the will depends on the complexity of what you leave and the detail with which you want to specify your precise wishes. There may be enough variations to fill many pages of single-spaced, typewritten, legal-

size paper (although presumably not as long as the will of a
widow of a London drapery manufacturer, probated in 1925,
that was 1,066 pages long, contained in four bound volumes).
Still, the permutations and combinations can be endless.

If there are minor children the will should specify their
guardian (your spouse, presumably, if you have one) and
also an alternative guardian in case both of you should die in
a common disaster. The children may also need a financial
guardian as well as a personal one if the money involved is
so great that "prudent management" of their inheritance is
required.

Adopted children must be given special attention. In some
states, although legally adopted, their inheritance status is
somewhat different from natural children, certainly so if one
of *your* children has adopted a child.

Many wills traditionally contain a clause specifying the
kind of funeral arrangements you'd like. While in the majority of cases the funeral will be over by the time the will is
formally read (in which case the instructions in the will are
of course null and void), presumably this clause is inserted
because your closest next of kin will have read the will before
you died or before the formal reading of the will in order
that the instructions can be carried out.

Should you have a personal attachment to anyone who is
not a blood relative or related by marriage and wish your
friend to take care of all funeral arrangements, *say so in the
will*. Find out what legal claims others such as a disapproving
family or an ex-spouse may have and if these people can be
expected to try to override your wishes. If so, get expert
legal help to anticipate and nullify such claims. Court challenges on this have not yet been definitive.

Complications relating to an ongoing business can result in
major dislocations. Preventing these is absolutely essential,

and the matter of reducing these dislocations—through insurance and discretionary policymaking powers of the executor —should receive closest attention when the will is drawn up.

Many wills contain clauses that disinherit anyone who contests the will or include language that requires the contestant to pay all court costs. Whether the last will hold up in all courts or not, the risk of possibly paying all litigation expenses should discourage any frivolous action.

Whatever instructions you include in the will, the provisions should not be so rigid and detailed as to prevent discretionary action by the executor if unforeseen circumstances arise. Don't try to control each and every conceivable condition. You chose that executor or executrix so you would have a person who could exercise good judgment and responsibility if such circumstances do arise. Give him or her leeway to do just that.

TRUSTS

A very important feature of your will can be its estate-conserving features, particularly testamentary trusts. Moderate-income persons as well as the wealthy are resorting to trusts with great frequency as a precaution against having the same property taxed not only one time, but a second and even a third time as it passes from the original owner to a spouse to the children. In addition, under good management a trustee can increase the income and substance of your assets for your heirs, provide built-in flexibility in the management of your estate, and control and preserve funds from the immaturity or irresponsibility of your heirs. This will be discussed in greater detail in a further chapter.

The will is concluded when it is properly signed and witnessed, with the correct addresses of the witnesses. At your death they may have to be summoned by the court so the will can be validated.

After the will is drawn up, put it away in a safe place. If it's drawn up by an attorney (and presumably it has been), the original copy should be kept in the attorney's files, and a duplicated copy should be held in a safe-deposit box at the bank, or in your desk. This is not because the safe-deposit box is so inaccessible when you die—an erroneous assumption—but rather to insure that the lawyer is notified immediately when you die. Since the practical problems your next of kin will face at your death are almost all legal and financial, the sooner the attorney is brought into the picture, the better for everyone concerned.

At periodic intervals the will must be reviewed to make certain the provisions are still viable. It certainly should be reviewed and possibly rewritten if there are changes in your family (a child is born or dies, a spouse dies) or changes take place in your property profile or your business, if a named executor dies or the witnesses are no longer available, and so on.

Make particularly sure you check over your will if you are moving to another state. While in general a will executed in one state is valid in another, sometimes it is not. In any case, it's usually better to have an executor (and perhaps even an attorney) situated in the locality you are moving to who knows local practices and who won't cause any undue delay or traveling expenses from out of state when the will is probated.

8

Providing a Financial Cushion: Insurance

To make your survivors' future without you as free from financial hardship as possible, you must do more than provide for an orderly and fair transfer of your assets through a will. Make sure you leave *enough*—or at least as much of a financial cushion as you can.

SOCIAL SECURITY

Fortunately, those who can't do more than provide for their dependents now no longer need worry that their survivors will be destitute, as before the 1930s. A vast publicly owned insurance system called social security (or more correctly, Old Age, Survivors' and Disability Insurance—OASDI) covers more than ninety percent of the labor force. In death-benefit terms, Consumers Union estimates that "OASDI can easily represent, among other things, $75,000 to $100,000 of decreasing term life insurance in a unique form. Each time a

75

child is born to an OASDI-insured father, the father's social security life insurance is restored to its maximum face value, and its term is automatically restored to a potential twenty-one years."

Since the amount of benefits your surivivors get depends to some degree on how much money has been credited to your social security account (the amount both contributed by your employer and deducted from your pay check), check at regular intervals with the main office of the Social Security Administration, Baltimore, Maryland, to find out how much this is. Send them a "Request for Statement of Earnings" postcard, obtained from your local social security office. If on the same card you say "Benefit estimate, please," they will compute for you the size and duration of the annuity your family may be entitled to if you should die during the next year. According to one social security operations manager, a request for a statement of earnings should be made at least once every three years. If you notice a discrepancy between what the SSA in Baltimore says you should have and the amount noted on your yearly W-2 form as having been reported by your employer, bring this irregularity immediately to the attention of the local office.

Application for survivors' benefits can only be made by a survivor. However, you can help him or her by making sure relevant documents are gathered in a readily accessible place. These should include your social security card stub, your most recent W-2 form or income tax return, a copy of your marriage certificate, possibly your own birth certificate and those of the children (if proof of age is relevant), and possibly your military discharge papers (to increase your insured status by giving credit for your service years).

LIFE INSURANCE

For the majority of Americans whose income consists of salaries and wages, life insurance is the principal means of providing for dependents after death. The face value of the insurance policies provides an "instant estate" to your survivors when the paycheck stops.

Life insurance can, and often does, serve other purposes as well. You can purchase insurance to provide a savings account, a source for low-interest loans, or a retirement income. You can also purchase it as part of an estate plan to minimize posthumous taxes, to pay off posthumous debts, to permit your business partners to buy out your heirs' share of the business, or to protect the assets of a closely held corporation to which you've devoted your working life.

LIFE INSURANCE AS DEATH-BENEFIT PROTECTION

But if the main purpose of your insurance is to provide your dependents with death benefits when you die, then you must concentrate on making sure that they get as much in death benefits as possible for the money you spend. With this perspective, all these "extras," which have value for other purposes, are simply side benefits as far as the death-benefit protection of the insurance is concerned. When you buy side benefits instead of straight life insurance, you run the risk of being badly underinsured—and most families are. If you carry $30,000 of life insurance, the average insurance a family has, this amount will last less than six years if invested at 4 percent at your death, even if your survivors are careful not to draw out more than $500 a month.

To understand life insurance protection as survivors' protection there are two basic principles to remember:

1. Life insurance is for people who have dependents relying on their financial support. If you are single, with no parents or children to support, or married to a financially independent spouse, with no parents or children to support, you have no need for life insurance. The money you earn is far better put into a savings account, toward a retirement income, given to charity, or spent on the tangibles of life to make living more pleasant for you and your family. (You may want to buy a small term policy to care for your burial and funeral until you have a savings account to do the same thing, but that's all.) You surely don't need this kind of protection if you're wealthy.

2. If you're the sole support of your dependents, then you and *only* you should be insured. Only the family wage earners —those who earn enough of an income that its loss would impair the family's standard of living—should carry insurance. Money shouldn't be diverted to insure children or an unemployed wife, except perhaps for a small decreasing term policy to take care of the short-term transition period if there are young children.

All life insurance is basically one of two types. One kind is term insurance, which is pure death-benefit protection and nothing else. The other type is cash-value insurance. Cash-value insurance includes ordinary whole life (also called straight life), limited-payment life, and endowment insurance (among others). They all combine insurance protection with a savings account. Cash-value insurance offers "something else" besides just insurance—a savings account, cash value, a monthly income and other features—and for this reason many people find it very attractive. But when the money is returned as any of these options is realized, the life insurance aspect is gone.

TERM INSURANCE

The most flexible, the least expensive, and the kind of insurance that gives the most death-benefit protection is renewable term insurance.

Level Renewable Term Insurance. Level renewable term insurance has a fixed death benefit, the amount of its face value. The premium you pay increases each time the term (one, five, or ten years) is renewed, and the premium increases until the age of 65 or 70. The company agrees not to require a medical examination as a condition of renewal. The only reason for cancelling the policy is because of the nonpayment of the premium.

Decreasing Renewable Term. Decreasing renewable term insurance has a fixed annual premium, but each time the insurance is renewed for another term the amount of insurance goes down. (This is similar to the term insurance you have covering the mortgage of a home.)

One advantage of term insurance is not often appreciated. By requiring you to renew your insurance at periodic intervals you are forced to check to see if you should decrease your coverage. (Hardly any company will let you *increase* the term insurance you now carry without an accompanying physical examination.) Insurance needs change. For a while, as you and your children grow older, your financial responsibilities rise. But eventually they taper off and decrease. Meanwhile your assets of cash, savings, and investment grow to take care of your retirement income and any medical expenses you and your spouse might incur. At that time you might consider dropping your term insurance altogether. With no other dependents to care for after you die, your only responsibility is to provide money to cover the expenses connected with your funerals.

Term insurance is also relatively inexpensive. If you bought, for example, a $50,000 policy of five-year renewable term insurance at the age of twenty-five, it might cost you only $195 a year. A $50,000 ordinary whole life insurance policy would cost $428 a year. Yet if you died shortly after paying the premium on either policy your survivors would get $50,000.

To put it another way, the $428 that bought $50,000 of whole ordinary life could have bought more than twice that amount of survivors' protection if it had been used to buy renewable term life insurance instead.

Of course if you already own life insurance the problem is different than if you were just going on the market to buy life insurance from scratch. You must evaluate the insurance you possess in terms of your other needs, which vary with your age, your affluence, your family's dependency on the death-benefit aspects alone, your need for the other benefits insurance offers, and so on. Getting the help of a good insurance broker to evaluate your present insurance and see what additional insurance can be bought to satisfy all your needs is becoming almost as important as having a lawyer or a physician to keep tabs on your legal or medical needs.

It is usually very unwise to drop any life insurance policy, particularly a cash-value one, to switch to another, even if the policy in force costs more. Cash values build up as the policy gets older and dividends usually get bigger each year. But if you do, the advice of the insurance experts is don't, repeat, *don't ever* drop any policy unless its replacement is signed, sealed, and delivered—and this means having passed the medical and all other requirements and having a receipt for the payment of the first premium.

How much insurance you should carry has become more

of an individual problem than in the past. At one time the rule-of-thumb was to carry three times your current income in life insurance. Now with insurance serving multiple needs, it is best to get a good insurance broker to review your requirements regularly to see how much you should carry.

As you get older, term life insurance premiums increase as the mortality table indicates chances of your dying increases. But the cost of buying new cash-value insurance also increases as you get older. And the likelihood of your developing a serious health problem, thereby making it difficult for you to get a cash-value policy involving a medical examination, will increase as well.

Ten years ago, if you had had a heart attack or diabetes or were operated on for cancer, you were uninsurable no matter *what* you were willing to pay for the insurance. This is no longer true. Today, depending on how good your agent is in finding a company that will carry it, you can get insurance, even at close to standard rates. But companies vary greatly as to whom they insure and on what terms.

Some companies offer coverage at initially high premiums but are willing to renew your policy after two or three years, after they review your case. If your health has improved, or if the state of the art in medicine has progressed in the treatment of your disorder, they will reduce your rate. Other companies will make a reduction to a standard rate automatic after maintaining a high rate for a fixed period of perhaps three to five years. But you have to look around for policies like these.

GROUP LIFE INSURANCE

The life insurance you buy on an individual basis isn't the only life insurance you may own. You may be covered by life insurance you don't know about; you may also be carrying some that you should increase. Make sure you check them out and add them in to your entire life insurance package.

Pension Trust Insurance. If you have a vested interest in a company pension or profit-sharing plan, the employer may have deposited some funds into a trust to buy life insurance on the lives of the employees participating in the plan. Either you or your life insurance agent should find out if there is such, how much it is, who is in charge of the insurance program, and how claim to the money is to be made.

On-the-Job Group Life Insurance. This is insurance offered by the company to all its employees with the employer paying part or all of the premium. Usually you have an option of taking as much or as little as you wish (above a certain minimum) at successive increments. Not only are the rates quite low, but the insurance can be gotten without a medical examination. As such it is a very good buy. In fact as you grow older and find yourself increasingly uninsurable for health reasons, you certainly should buy all the group life insurance available to you on the job. It usually can be converted to ordinary life without a medical examination if you leave the company—however, based on your increased age, it will be at a higher premium.

Some companies now offer a type of group insurance known as group ordinary, which combines ordinary life insurance with group insurance. The company pays the group rate; you pay the difference between the group rate and level, ordinary life. Besides accruing cash-value benefits while you're with the company, if you should leave, the premiums on the ordinary life insurance you would pay are lower than they would be calculated as new insurance at your present age.

Association or Other Group Term Insurance. Various professional, alumni, and special interest groups now offer group insurance to their members, and when the group is large, the rates are frequently low. This, too, should be taken advantage of as often as possible; there's a lot of death-benefit protection offered in such policies at relatively low cost.

INSURANCE TIPS

Check over your insurance policy beneficiaries with your agent to make sure they don't conflict with the beneficiaries you've listed in your will. Don't let your heirs get short-changed through your inadvertent oversight. The insurance money must be paid to the beneficiaries as noted on the policy, not as listed in the will.

Also check out the policies to see whether you've specified any particular settlement option, that is, the manner in which insurance proceeds are to be distributed to your beneficiary. You may want to, of course, for reasons of your own, but as a general rule, try not to lay down stipulations so stringent that survivors' interests are jeopardized if circumstances change. For if you do, the insurance company must treat the option you name like a Last Will and Testament, possibly to your survivors' disadvantage.

Also ask your agent if you can insert language into the policy that will permit the beneficiary to take out a limited loan against the principal (presuming the money is not drawn out in one lump sum) in case of a temporary need for a large sum of money.

LIFE INSURANCE AS AN ESTATE-PLANNING DEVICE

Life insurance in estate planning has been employed by the wealthy for many years. Even if you are in the middle-income brackets you may find it an excellent tool for conserving wealth for your dependents. It can be as valuable in dollars and cents to them as the death-benefit life insurance you now carry.

Using life insurance in this way is definitely *not* a do-it-yourself project. But in the hands of an experienced attorney who understands the device it is invaluable. It should certainly be very seriously considered when your will, or a trust for your survivors, is under consideration. A good insurance agent and tax attorney working together can appreciably increase your estate this way for your heirs. Get their help as part of a complete estate-planning program.

9

Providing a Financial Cushion: Estate Conservation

For most families with no other income than the wage-earner's salary, the possibility of meeting all future needs by insurance and social security alone is poor. If the wage earner should die, it may appear that the only course open is for the spouse to get a job quickly, while paring back the family standard of living to as spartan a level as possible.

This is not necessarily true. There are other alternatives open to everyone. Many people have more to their estate than they realize. You may be part of a union welfare plan or a company profit-sharing plan from which your survivors will get substantial annuities. You may have equity wealth now that can be converted into income by your survivors (a house that can be sold and the proceeds invested at a good return). You may own income-producing property such as real estate and securities, which expand your estate.

How to develop these supplements into wealth now is beyond the scope of this book. But how to preserve what you *do* have or will have when you die, in order to leave your survivors more, is pertinent here.

You must be concerned now to see that the wealth you own is not dissipated in the transfer process. The following highlights the main areas of concentration.

AVOIDING PROBATE

One of the avenues open to you, surprisingly, is aimed at keeping the assets away from the government branch ostensibly set up to protect your heirs: the probate courts. Tax lawyers groan at this advice—but both legal and lay opinion is just as strong in its support.

As mentioned earlier, the delays and expense accompanying the probate process have often been so noticeable (according to some critics so notorious) that even persons with modest incomes may find it worthwhile to own their property in such a way that the probate process is bypassed as much as possible.

One device frequently used—joint tenancy with right of survivorship—has often been called "the poor man's will." Real property or personal property such as bank accounts, stocks, bonds, or an automobile can be owned by two or more persons during their lifetimes, with the provision that a surviving owner retains rights to all the property remaining after the death of the others. Property held in this way doesn't negate the need for a will; it just passes the property to the surviving owner no matter *what* is in the will. Just make certain the wording of the ownership clause fits the law of your state.

Funds that transfer to named beneficiaries also pass outside the probate process. These include United States savings bonds, pension benefits and annuities, and life insurance.

The increasing use of *inter vivos* (living) trusts as devices for avoiding probate is discussed later in this chapter.

ESTATE PLANNING

A major step is to embark on a total estate-planning program to conserve your wealth by using trusts, insurance, gifts, or income-splitting devices to keep the tax impact as low as possible.

Usually any discussion about avoiding taxes sounds both esoteric and elitist to people who never considered themselves wealthy enough to apply such measures to *their* estates. After all, federal estates taxes are of consequence only if the estate of a single person is more than $60,000, or if the estate is $120,000 if the deceased was married and leaves a surviving spouse to claim the remaining $60,000 as a community property or marital deduction.

But these figures are deceiving. These amounts are not as huge as they appear, and state taxes can be of consequence when the estate is only $20,000—or even less. Since your gross estate includes everything you own including insurance, this ceiling is soon reached. If you and your spouse have equity in a $50,000 house, the equity can appreciate quickly through inflation alone to a taxable level. Property held in joint tenancy is included in your gross estate at its full market value, unless your spouse can later prove that half of it was actually bought with her or his own money, not yours. If you have a business, or have accumulated stocks over the years, or if you own real property—even if it's just a few acres in the country —you're already at an income level where ways to cut down the tax may be important. Bonds exempt from tax for the survivor are not exempted from being considered part of the gross estate for taxing purposes.

Still you may feel slightly uneasy at the idea of manipulating your holdings to avoid taxes. Be assured that the effort to keep taxes down is not only perfectly legal but proper as well. No less distinguished a jurist than the late Justice Learned Hand observed many years ago that there was nothing wrong in doing so:

> Over and over again courts have said that there is nothing sinister in so arranging one's affairs as to keep taxes as low as possible. Everybody does it, rich or poor, and all do right, for nobody owes any public duty to pay more than the law demands. Taxes are enforced exactions, not voluntary contributions. To demand more in the name of morals is mere cant.

Estate planning has been a preoccupation of the wealthy for many years. Its advantages are just becoming clear to persons of more modest incomes. If the words themselves seem to have a patrician ring to them, think of it simply as figuring out how to leave your dependents as much as possible of what you own, without any leakage to persons you don't know and don't particularly care to share your wealth with in preference to your heirs.

Estate planning is definitely not a do-it-yourself project. While estate planning is considered when drawing up your will, it's not the same as writing a will. Though the attorney who draws up the will knows the various principles involved to protect your estate, you should also consult other experts. In this area expert advice is of incomparable value. An insurance agent, the trust officer at the bank or trust company, the tax lawyer, an accountant—all can advise you on working out the best arrangement.

Basically you have two alternative ways to leave your possessions to your survivors: either outright to one or more heirs, or in a trust for their benefit. These can be used separately or jointly to get the best mix for your particular circumstances, in a flexible process that is not simple or cut-and-dried. Some of the techniques used, for example, are:

• The use of gifts to individuals, either outright or in trust, because of generous gift tax exemptions. This can save estate taxes considerably.

• The use of charitable gifts, either outright or by trust, to save on estate and gift taxes.

• The special disposition of such benefits to your survivors as pension payments or profit-sharing returns for tax-saving purposes.

• The establishment of a trust as an alternative to an outright distribution of assets after death. Some trust officers feel that trusts are worth considering if you earn over $15,000, own some real estate, and have some insurance or company benefits.

A trust is an arrangement for transferring part or all of your property to another person or corporation (called the trustee) to hold or manage it according to your instructions, for your own benefit or a third party.

A trust can be either a testamentary trust or a living trust. The first goes into effect when you die and is incorporated in your will. This is set up for the benefit of that other party, your heirs.

The second, an *inter vivos* or living trust, begins to operate during your lifetime as soon as you set it up and continues after your death without a break. If the living trust is irrevocable, set up for the benefit of your heirs, it incorporates many liberal tax advantages. If it's revocable, there are many fewer tax advantages, but it then has all the flexibility of a will, since it can be amended or cancelled at any time before your death.

Unlike a testamentary trust, which is part of the will and presented for probate, the living trust bypasses the probate process entirely, avoiding the delays and costs of probate, and, an interesting bonus, it also keeps the affairs of the estate private, away from the public eye. These advantages can be quite substantial. The living trust is favored not only by corporate trust officers but by many consumer-oriented critics of the probate system.

Living trusts also have another subtle advantage. For those who fear making a will, it allows them to accomplish the same objective without actually sitting down and making a will as such.

A testamentary trust also serves many useful purposes. Preventing redundant taxation is one. Another is allowing competent trustees to manage assets of your estate that the survivors themselves are incapable of managing (as in the case of a physically or mentally incapacitated child or spouse, or a dependent parent who eventually may become incapacitated and require nursing home or institutional care), and to do this with judgment and flexibility.

A little less commendable is your use of the trust for paternalistic or maternalistic, but presumably good, reasons to give you cautionary control beyond the grave over the way your dependents handle the assets you leave them. Through the trust, for example, you can give them an income from property without permitting them access to the principal until such time (if ever) as they are capable of handling the money on their own.

The specialized trust, both testamentary and living, can be in the form of an insurance trust, an educational trust, a multiple trust, a fringe-benefit trust, a sprinkling trust. All have possible uses for income-splitting and other goals in all income brackets.

To explore the possibilities, you and your spouse should arrange to see a trust officer of a reputable bank or trust company (there is little difference between the two). At this point the advice of the officers of either institution is free. However, once the trust is set up and they become the trustees, the trust institution charges an annual fee, usually around 1 percent of the trust's assets. Thus the advantages of setting up a trust must be weighed against what may turn out to be a continuing cost, possibly for many years.

Then consult your estate attorney and organize your affairs for the future.

DOCUMENTATION

If part of your estate eventually will be probated, a simple but enormously useful step to save money is to organize your records and documents as completely as you possibly can now while you're alive.

This is particularly important if the estate is small rather than large, because the time spent in searching out even small but hard-to-locate property may be great—and for the small estates the cost represents a larger percentage than that charged the big estate. The executor's time saved is translated immediately into dollar savings for the estate that could be considerable.

Documentation is the paper foundation on which the entire house of our financial and legal existence is based. For your survivors' sake, draw up an inventory of all the information they will need. Gather the papers together, if you have them, or make careful notations as to where the papers are to be found and what they contain.

FINANCIAL INVENTORY

A financial inventory may have been required before, perhaps as part of your income tax return, as the basis for a personal loan at a bank, or in a request for financial assistance from the college of your child's choice. Your attorney may have asked for one in drawing up your will. Perhaps you're simply an organized person who does this sort of thing automatically.

Most books on estate planning list what should be included, breaking down in detail what is required in each of the many categories. A fairly comprehensive checklist is found in Section II of a postmortem tabulation, "Putting My House In Order," put out by the Continental Association of Funeral and Memorial Societies, Washington, D.C. The federal estate tax form indicating the broad categories also gives a framework to work with. As a last resort, if you have no other handy inventory form, check with your local bank. They usually have forms that will help you collate these data.

The inventory lists and financial and legal papers should be kept in a place where both your attorney and executor can get at them. The safe deposit box at the bank is fine.

The property to be inventoried should be listed with all identifying information: what, where, when, how much, with whom, from whom; and all relevant file, code, and account numbers. The list should include all real property, owned jointly or separately (particularly out-of-state property); stocks and bonds, mutual fund shares, debentures; mortgages and notes; life insurance, both on yourself and on others of which you're a beneficiary, and all other insurance (disability, medical, casualty); checking accounts, saving accounts in banks, savings-and-loan and credit-union accounts, and also cash equivalents; annuities and pensions; valuable personal property including title to boats, cars, or trailers; and business interests not listed elsewhere. Accompanying this should be a list of all your liabilities, including any lawsuits or claims against you, with relevant data.

PERSONAL RECORDS

These are required as proof for many claims: your birth certificate or baptismal certificate; marriage license; divorce decree, if any; social security card stub; naturalization papers, if any; military discharge papers; deed to family cemetery lot; passport; health records; birth certificates of children; death certificates of any members of the family; membership of various lodges; membership in professional or business-related organizations.

NAMES AND ADDRESSES

A list of people whom your spouse or survivors may have to call in the case of your death should be kept in the house. It should list the name, address, phone number (very important) of your attorney, executor (if other than spouse), banker, clergyman, doctor, employer, stock broker, insurance agents (life, car, household property, health), union official in charge of union death benefits or union-administered pension funds, company official in charge of group insurance or the profit-sharing plan, lodge representative, the closest social security office, the closest Veterans Administration office, and helpful neighbors. Of course, your companion or spouse will have a list of close relatives and their phone numbers and addresses elsewhere.

Another surprisingly important list is one of names that you know but others might not know: the present married name of your ex-spouse, the married names of your children of a former marriage, names and addresses of family friends or relatives you've never really lost total contact with but haven't seen for a long time, and anyone else you feel may want to be informed at your death.

PART II

Special Decisions When Death Is Imminent

10

Preparing for Your Own Death

If you develop a terminal illness, the last thing you probably want to discuss, at the beginning anyway, is what will happen after you are dead. The problem of dying seems, at times, all that you can manage. In your anger you may feel you couldn't care less about what happens later; you won't be around anyway.

But as you think about it, you know this isn't true. After having willingly shouldered the responsibility for your dependents' welfare for so many years, it's unlikely you'd choose to abandon them now, particularly since the details you take care of now can mean the difference between a relatively easy transition and a frantic dislocation that can stretch on for years.

The words of a patient who participated in a Death and Dying Seminar held at the University of Chicago recently seem applicable. When the chaplain asked him how he found the strength to face up to the fact of his death, he said:

I don't know. I don't think you find the strength in anything. It's just something that has to be done. If anything happens to me I realize that she and the family will have to be taken care of. I have reminded my wife what kind of insurance I have. I've changed the title of the car—all things that would help her in the end. It's not so much a matter of strength, it's more like something that you've got to face up to. Obligations are obligations, that's all.

FUNERAL AND BURIAL ARRANGEMENTS

Have you taken care of these before you became ill? If not, you might ask your spouse, closest friend, or attorney to make them now rather than waiting. It isn't the money; there won't be any savings any more. (You can still join a funeral or memorial society, but the time for shopping around for a less expensive mortuary is past.) But you can still give suggestions.

Possibly you and your spouse have no difficulty talking about this subject at all. In that case, have her or him make whatever funeral and burial or cremation arrangements are necessary.

But if talking about funerals is hard, if you find you simply cannot initiate a conversation about such things, then don't press it. Maybe the family isn't quite up to facing it either. Instead, put your thoughts down on paper. Write a letter to your spouse or child, or "to whom it may concern." It's not to be mailed to anyone; it will be put into an envelope to be opened later.

You may need help from the nurse if you can't write too well, or if your thoughts have a tendency to wander. She in turn may have to get the physician's approval, and they may come up with reasons why you mustn't exert yourself. Insist if you have to. It's your right and it's important.

Keep the letter informal, putting down in writing instructions about the funeral or memorial service you'd like. Perhaps there's one particular friend you'd like to speak, or a clergyman to give the eulogy. Is there any favorite music you want played, or favorite passages read? Friends may want to send flowers. Indicate if that's all right or whether you'd prefer they contribute to a memorial fund you set up or to their favorite charity.

If you want to be cremated, do your spouse and other relatives know? If not, mention it in the letter, and tell them whether you want memorialization in a columbarium or just a scattering of your ashes in a garden or at sea.

If you own a family plot, then burial space is not a problem. If not, mention where you'd like to be buried and anything about the location that seems important to you.

Talk about the money involved if you care to. Maybe when you were well and detached from it all you once complained about the high cost of death, but now you have a different view of the matter. If so, say so, even if it contradicts funeral or cremation arrangements you have on file somewhere. This letter will alter those prior arrangements.

Or perhaps you feel just the opposite. Maybe it's been a family custom to have an elaborate funeral—but you hate to think of your survivors spending all that money on a funeral when it could be used for their ongoing expenses. Say so in the letter; it may divert some family criticism later when your wishes are honored.

If you have a more spiritual or personal statement to make, do it elsewhere, not in this letter. Strangers will be reading it, your attorney and the funeral director, among others. Confine your remarks to instructions about mundane things.

Don't worry if you haven't covered everything or haven't expressed any of it too well. The main thing is that it's there. Now others will have a guide of sorts to follow.

Put the letter in an envelope, write on the outside simply "Letter of Instructions" or "My Wishes," and put it aside. You can now put the matter out of your mind.

DISPOSING OF YOUR PROPERTY

Do everything you can to nail this down now. Concerning death and property, the law's strictures are like handcuffs: They're rigid as steel and cannot be undone until the official turns the key. Your survivors' difficulties will range from annoying to horrendous unless you do what you can to prevent your estate from becoming enmeshed in court technicalities and governmental red tape.

Make a will. If you haven't done so, you must; it's essential. Ask your spouse or friend to send you an attorney. Again, you will have to clear the visit with your physician or other health-care personnel who may find medical objections to your efforts. You may have to insist.

If there's property of any consequence in the estate, make sure you get the best attorney possible—even if it's at the expense of offending a close friend who may be a mediocre lawyer. At this point, cutting corners on legal fees is like worrying about a leaky faucet when the water main is about to burst.

Make a will even if you think you don't have much wealth to leave. If nothing else, it will get you to think about how much you *do* have, things you may have forgotten about: a piece of property you've been paying taxes on but have done nothing about; the odd-lot stocks you've accumulated over the years which may or may not be worth anything; that Swiss clock left by grandfather that someone told you was a valuable antique.

Tell the attorney where your safe deposit box is located, where the key is kept, who else has access to it, and generally what's in it so that it may be checked, with your permission, as part of making a financial and legal inventory. Also tell the attorney where your income tax returns are kept or how to get in touch with your accountant; they may have to work together quickly. It's too late now to give away any part of your estate to save federal estate taxes; but your attorney may have suggestions on how gifts now can still save money.

Consider all matters mentioned in previous chapters about what to include in the will. Some actions are no longer feasible. As for others, instruct your attorney to act on them immediately. Getting instruments written, typed up, and properly signed, witnessed and/or notarized is time consuming—and time is valuable now.

Do you want to change the beneficiaries of your insurance? Is a transfer of stock from joint ownership to your spouse alone still feasible? Can you still get a trust agreement properly executed? or out-of-state property liquidated? If none of these is possible anymore, simply alerting the attorney to problems that may arise is useful.

Have the will properly signed and properly witnessed as expeditiously as possible. Tell the attorney to keep the original, or give it to your family lawyer (if it's someone else). Give a copy to one of your survivors to put away. Then put the matter out of your mind. It's one more responsibility you've discharged.

MAKING THE FINANCIAL TRANSITION EASIER

If you've already put your financial house in order, simply tell your survivors or the attorney where the papers and documents are. If you haven't, tell them where the papers are to be found and ask one of them to make an inventory now, so you can help while you're able.

Find out from the attorney how to shift the money in your checking and savings accounts so ready cash is available to your survivors immediately. Transfer the registration of your car over to your spouse or whomever you choose as beneficiary. If not, at least sign the registration slip so the car can be sold without difficulty if need be.

Make sure the beneficiary of your U.S. savings bonds is correct. Have your spouse or child rent another safe deposit box and transfer whatever she or he wants from yours into the new one. Also be sure that whatever instructions or documents he or she will need to make claim to insurance or death-benefit payments have been removed.

As a final assist, make a list of all the people your survivors will need to give help later on, as outlined at the end of the previous chapter.

GET YOUR INSURANCE IN ORDER

It would appear too late to get any more life insurance— but maybe not. Talk with a top-notch life insurance agent or broker (have the attorney find one) to see what still can be done. It may be possible to get a special kind of life insurance policy, obtainable regardless of your physical condition. There are policies like this in which you can't lose: They become true life insurance if you survive the test period (which varies). Otherwise, if you should die before then, your survivors receive the premiums you've already paid in. The premiums will be very high, of course, but it surely would be worth looking into. (This type of policy can be obtained only in certain states.)

Ask the insurance agent if even at this late date you can still increase your coverage under your company group plan. Even if there isn't much extra you can get, a small additional amount may help.

Check your present life insurance to see if the beneficiaries are correct. If not, change them without delay. Delegate to the agent the job of checking out company-held or union-held insurance, tracking down the name, title, and phone number of the person your survivor must contact to make a claim.

BUSINESS MATTERS

If you're the sole owner of a business, tidy up your affairs, and think through carefully what you want to have happen to the business when you die. If you're in business with others, it's of utmost urgency to get these matters straightened out immediately. Your associates may be uncomfortable talking about "closing" matters, even though they've been visiting you regularly and talking about business in general. Put them at their ease if you can, but don't let their reluctance prevent you from discussing with them what will happen to your shares, who will take over in your place, and what the role of your survivors will be when you die. Unless you do it now, all you've worked for all these years may be lost and your survivors' financial future may be in serious jeopardy. So see that your attorney and your business associates face the issue now.

PERSONAL MATTERS

As death draws closer, there may be matters never before mentioned that must be brought out into the open. Your spouse, children, or attorney must know about them for reasons more compelling than just a matter of clearing your conscience.

St. Matthew said it first, but lawyers, police officers, and all tax collectors say amen to the statement: "Nothing is secret, that shall be made manifest." Never do secrets break out into the open more quickly than when death occurs.

While the probate process ordinarily is just a routine matter, it is a public one. If you are wealthy, or newsworthy, or sometimes for no reason at all, your death will come to the attention of many people, and the ripple effect travels to faraway shores.

Your business, professional, and financial affairs will be thoroughly checked by tax agents and your executor. All unexplained bills or financial obligations will have to be checked out, including such things as pawn tickets, keys to public lockers, and claim checks to safes in strange hotels— and these may cause complications.

For example, if you've been caring for a deranged aunt or a mentally deficient child by an earlier marriage without anyone's knowledge, it will become known when the sanitarium bills or receipts show up. An unresolved AWOL conviction from World War I may surface when your survivor contacts the VA for the funeral and burial allowance.

More serious secrets can jeopardize your dependents' future, certainly their peace of mind. If a long-forgotten, never properly dissolved marriage once took place, the appearance of a wife or child may cast doubt on your present spouse's entire inheritance. A brother challenging the validity of your will may reveal a hidden history of psychiatric treatment your survivors never knew about. Better bring all these out now, to your attorney if not to your spouse and children, otherwise they'll find out later in an unpleasant, public way.

Perhaps generous motives may cause trouble: the payment of the college expenses of a niece or nephew against parental wishes, for example. Let someone know about it now; it may prevent a complete rupture in family relations that will take place if those regular repayment checks from the niece or nephew come to light.

With this, you've tidied all the obligations you owe those you love. Now let others take over the responsibility.

II

Preparing for a Death in the Family

Someone you love is dying: your spouse, a parent, a friend with whom you've shared your life for many years. He or she still appears to hope that the death sentence is not final, although the doctor has told you both that the prognosis is very bad.

Each day, with every visit, you watch the struggle, the refusal to consider the inevitable. Maybe this denial of reality is an example of a bad mental attitude, as some say. But perhaps there's another explanation. Maybe, through this nonrecognition, the one you love is asserting to everyone, including him- or herself, that no human being should be laid low by a malignancy that makes a travesty of all human dignity. And maybe, by the very denial, he or she is able to withstand the assaults of the disease better than by supine acquiescence. Be that as it may, soon the day will arrive when the disease will wreak its worst and death will come. Then what?

FUNERAL AND BURIAL ARRANGEMENTS

If the two of you made plans earlier about the funeral and burial, then at least that unpleasant task is done. If you belong to a memorial society or have made private arrangements with a mortician, when the time comes you only need call up the mortuary who will take care of everything as pre-arranged.

If not, perhaps you can ask close friends or relatives to make the arrangements for you. Give them some idea of what you would like and perhaps a money ceiling. Even if the arrangements turn out not to be exactly what you want, you can talk to the mortician after the death occurs and make any necessary changes. The important thing is that it will be done: the cemetery lot bought, the funeral arranged, the casket purchased.

If nothing has been done and no one else is around to do it but you, then the sooner you do it, the better, if only to get it out of the way before the full impact of grief hits you. It's a death chore that's no good to do at any time.

If the dying person refuses to talk about it, do what you feel is necessary. Check into the will (if you can locate it) to see if there are any funeral instructions in it. Look through the papers in the desk or the safe deposit box (if you have a joint key) for a letter of instruction. If you can find no guidelines, take an educated guess and make whatever arrangements seem best.

If medical bills are high, you'll certainly be aware of the price tag of death, too. But it's too late now to consider shopping around for bargains, even if you have the fortitude for it. At this point, you're already going through a period of anticipatory bereavement. As in the actual bereavement, you'll find your judgments are dulled, your temper and patience short, your attention drifting, and your mood not one that lends itself to any protracted mortuary or cemetery bargaining. Do what you must and be done with it.

THE WILL

The mortuary arrangements, unfortunately, may not be the worst thing you have to cope with. The major problems ahead involve legal and financial matters that begin their inexorable march as soon as the death occurs. Where property is concerned, the most heartless mortician is beneficence itself compared to that implacable, anonymous behemoth called The Law. And the prospect of what can happen once your loved one dies must make you consider drastic measures, doing what you'd rather avoid more than anything else.

If a will has not been made, somehow or other it will have to be done now. The problem is compounded if it's a parent who is dying, rather than a friend or spouse. If your mother or father is so angry as to refuse even to countenance the fact of death, surely he or she will consider the will as none of your business. If you broach the subject you'll be accused of grave-digging, ingratitude, interference, and insolence. You may have to listen to this in silence, even as you remember how once there was nothing the two of you couldn't at least discuss with understanding and openness.

It will be tempting to avoid the issue by saying: "It's his money. Let him do what he wants with it." The trouble is you know that if your parent—or your spouse—dies without a will, what will happen is *not* what he wants. If he were well, under no circumstances would he have consented to have his hard-earned money go to court-appointed strangers rather than to you, or the children, or the grandchildren, or

favorite charities. Each day you see how the pain and depres-
sion of the illness makes the dying patient strike out in contrary ways, by petty splurges of large gifts to casual hospital
personnel while refusing to sign a check to pay for needed
therapy or a private nurse, or with maudlin remorse for not
having made any provision for distributing property, coupled with sly lies to cover up the fact that he or she has no
intention of doing so voluntarily, today or tomorrow.

You cannot cope with this alone. You must get a lawyer
to come in and suggest in no uncertain terms that a will be
written immediately. Preferably it will be someone who is
correct but not particularly sympathetic. Preferably it will be
someone who is neither offended nor disturbed by threats of
violence or suicide, foul language or stubborn silences, by
hysteria or violent medical reactions. Presumably you must
get the aid of the doctor on this; the patient will use the
dying condition as an ultimate weapon. When the patient
appears so ill that he or she can no longer be restrained, the
attorney must leave, only to come back the following day.

The will must be made, signed, and witnessed, even if it
turns out to be a most unpleasant task of gargantuan proportions.

But keep the effort in perspective. If you *know* the inheritance is small and likely to be used up by doctor and
hospital bills, then don't bother. There's no point in pressing
the matter.

From now on, after the will ordeal is over, you must manage on your own. Check through papers at home to find out
if there's any insurance. If there is, gather the policies together
and prepare for the time when you must make a claim. Do
what you can about gathering together all legal documents:
property deeds, stock certificates, savings account books, and
so forth. Collect identification records: marriage certificate,

birth certificate, military record, etc. Enlist the help of the attorney to straighten out business matters if it can be done without the cooperation (obviously not forthcoming) from the patient.

You are now in the holding pattern; your bereavement has already begun. It's just a matter of time, waiting for the hour when death gratefully takes place.

PART III

Coping with a Death in the Family

12

Death As It Really Is

The fact is that Americans know very little about death as it really is, and we are almost completely innocent of knowing what to do when there is a death in the family. How could it be otherwise? The average American experiences death in the close family rarely, perhaps once in twenty years according to one writer. It seems the only death experiences we have are vicarious—through newspaper facts and TV fiction—and these appear so bizarre they tell us nothing about death as it will occur in our uneventful, mundane lives.

Millions of us have never experienced the loss of anyone close to us, or even been to a funeral. Sociologist Robert Fulton says we now have amongst us in the United States the first death-free generation in the world.

Not having had experience with the death of someone close to us, we have no precedents to guide us in what to do, with whom to deal, what the law requires, what the church requires, even what customary behavior to expect of our friends or the professionals who are supposed to know. Worst of all, we don't know whom to ask what to do because no one we know has ever talked about death.

Our confusion is compounded by the fact that today there are no longer any cut-and-dried answers. Even if we locate those who have coped with death, their experiences in handling religious or legal matters may no longer be pertinent if these took place even so recently as ten years ago.

Traditional mores that once regulated postdeath behavior have eroded so that few hard-and-fast guidelines remain for us to follow. The common-law presumption of kinship on which state inheritance statutes and regulatory agencies' postdeath benefits are based no longer stand unchallenged, as accepted but atypical family and living arrangements increase. In fact, an individual's right to make contractual arrangements that bridge death, once only applied to property, now is being expanded to include an exclusive right to control how one's body may be disposed of, and by whom. New case law challenges long-established legal precedents.

How to cope with a death in the *family* is, however, the concern of most Americans today. For while the legality of nonkinship relationships regarding postdeath rights is an expanding area of litigation, as yet it is an unresolved one and its ramifications vary from state to state. Since the rulings continue to change within each state and from state to state, few useful guidelines can be given at this time. The following chapters are, by and large, directed to survivors related by blood or marriage; often it is from the point of view of the surviving member of a married couple, although the advice may apply to other kin as well. At specific points, the matter of other interested survivors will be given.

Today, natural death comes primarily to middle-aged and older adults, certainly the elderly. The incidence of death by poliomyelitis, diphtheria, whooping cough, influenza—the killer of the young so prevalent two generations ago—has plummeted. In contrast, the incidence of fatal heart attacks, of carcinoma mortality, of the debilitating ravages of old age ending in viral pneumonia death, has risen sharply.

The death details and death-related problems that ensue must be taken care of by young adults, male and female, if it's the death of a parent; or by middle-aged wives (according to the mortality table), if it's the death of a husband. Most young adults know nothing about dealing with the business or ritual of the funeral and burial. Their experience in handling the postdeath legal matters and financial affairs involved, particularly when it involves the business or professional lives of their parents, is also almost nil, although their repertoire of expertise in handling affairs of their own is very useful.

The older wife may have more maturity, but in matters of death-related problems, she's as innocent as the adult twenty years her junior. Her knowledge of death in the family very likely is limited to that of her own parents, and it's quite possible she had nothing to do with arranging the funeral or settling the postdeath details then. So now, when faced with the death of her spouse, the desperation such ignorance triggers is very great indeed.

In order to cope adequately with death in the family, survivors must know what to anticipate when an expected or unexpected death takes place, how to make funeral and burial arrangements, what to expect by way of funeral rites, how to arrange for interim living funds, how to apply for postdeath benefits and claims, and how to settle the financial property affairs of the one who died.

This, and more, will be covered in the following nine chapters.

13

The Expected Death: Immediate Steps

Of the approximately 1,933,000 deaths in the United States in 1974, about 75 percent were by natural causes, the death certificate being signed by the attending physician. Many of these occurred in a hospital or nursing home after a long illness; only a comparatively small number took place in the home. What follows presumes that the expected death takes place in a health-care facility .

When death takes place, if you are present in the room, call the medical personnel at once. They will know what to do.

But if you are not there, you will be called either by the doctor or the nurse and asked to come to the hospital or home at once (which you will surely want to do anyway). After you say your final good-bys, you probably will be asked by the physician if an autopsy can be performed. If you agree, they'll ask you to sign a paper giving such permission. Ordinarily teaching hospitals like to perform as many autopsies as possible for the benefit of the residents and research workers. Most survivors acquiesce if this is a contribution to the store of medical knowledge which eventually can save lives. Most major religions have no objections (although Orthodox Judaism does not approve of autopsy for a frivolous purpose, and the dissection of the body by medical students is often so considered). The autopsy will not interfere with plans for open-casket viewing, although it may delay the viewing and the funeral a few days.

The hospital will also ask you to sign a release to permit them to remove the body from the room and prepare it for release to a mortuary. They will ask you also to call a mortuary of your choice.

Except for two special exceptions a mortuary must be called to take charge of a body. The first exception is if the body is to be donated to a medical school and state law permits the school to pick up the body as soon as the death certificate has been signed. The second occurs in those states that permit crematory personnel, not themselves licensed morticians, to come to the hospital to remove the body. (There are also instances of religious sects which pick up their dead and bury them as a community act, but these are very rare.)

If the body is to be donated to a medical school, you as closest next of kin should have been briefed as to the procedure to follow (since schools do not usually accept a gift of a body unless a predeath form has been signed by the donor). Usually you call the number of the medical school you've been given and an ambulance will be sent to the hospital. However, if you've arranged to donate the body after the funeral, then you simply notify the school about the death, and tell them that the mortician will call to get further instructions about embalming. In case the school tells you they have all the bodies they can use at this time (a frequent phenomenon in the Far West), you must then call a mortician and proceed in the customary manner.

If you have a mortuary already picked out and want them to come to the hospital immediately, the hospital or nursing home must release the body. They cannot "hold the body hostage," as it were, for unpaid medical bills or room-and-board payments due. Such a practice is clearly illegal.

However, the reverse is more likely to be true. Instead of insisting on holding the body, the nursing home, more frequently than a hospital, may insist that the body be removed as *quickly* as possible. Such places often lack adequate refrigeration facilities or even an empty cool room to keep the body for any length of time. They will be particularly insistent if they feel the body kept in sight of other patients has a deleterious effect on everyone in the home. And should they have difficulty locating the attending doctor, the attendants there might want to call the county hospital to have the body pronounced dead and removed to the county morgue.

Your only resort is to demand your right as next of kin to have the body removed only by the mortuary of your choice. You should not be panicked this way into choosing a mortician who is not the right one. (But it helps all around if you can get one without protracted delay.)

Immediately following the death, you may find yourself completely grief-stricken. On the other hand, if the death was expected, you may be frightened by your lack of grief. Other than the transient pain at the moment of hearing about the death, you may find no emotion so strong as a marked sense of relief. Realize that you're not a monster; perhaps you are in shock and realization of the death will hit you later. Or perhaps your grief was all worked out long before the death took place; you've been grieving for many months, or weeks, or years—there simply are no more tears left.

The first thing you must do is decide which funeral director to call. If you belong to a funeral or cremation society or have made prior private arrangements with a mortuary, call them; the mortuary will get in touch with the hospital and arrange to pick up the body. Because arrangement plans are already on file at the mortuary, a single phone call ordinarily puts the agreed-upon procedure into motion.

When the person who died entered the hospital, the hospital personnel asked for the name of a mortuary. It occasionally happens that he or she gave them the name of a mortuary with which all the funeral details had been prearranged without your knowledge. After the death takes place and the hospital or nursing home alerts this mortician (after notifying you of the death), the mortician will get in touch with you to tell you that everything has already been taken care of.

One Los Angeles mortician explains what then happens. "When we call, the family is usually relieved to find out that the arrangements have already been made. We'll ask if they want us to send a car for them to come to the funeral home. Often all they have to do is set a date and time for the service. If, for example, it was their mother, we tell them what she wanted, which minister, all the details of the funeral. We frequently have all the vital statistics we need for the death certificate. Perhaps the only extra thing we need to ask the family about is how many certified copies of the death certificate they need; and we obtain them for their use."

But if the one who died had not given the hospital the name of a funeral home and you must now make a choice, don't act in haste. You don't have to make up your mind as quickly as is customarily presumed. Most hospitals will keep a body twenty-four hours or more if you ask them to, perhaps at a small extra charge, to give you a little more time to make a wise decision.

First, see if you can find out if mortuary arrangements have already been made with a local mortician. Look around among his or her papers to see if you can find any contract or a name to show this has been done. Sometimes parents take out a funeral account giving the name of a particular local funeral home as beneficiary—but they don't pass on the name to the hospital, or you. (They may have forgotten or didn't think at the time it was relevant.) In fact, all or part of the mortician's fee may already have been taken care of. Even spouses have been known to make such arrangements in secret. Unless you find the name now, you may make arrangements with another home and have to collect the prepaid money later.

If no mortuary has been chosen, you must make a decision on your own. It's the choosing of a funeral home and the negotiation regarding the funeral and casket so soon after the death takes place, when the grief is still paramount, that survivors often find so distressing. They feel too vulnerable to extraneous pressures. At times like this, organized committees within some churches stand ready to take over. Recently two instances of church activity on behalf of congregants immediately after death takes place were discussed on a Chicago public television program on the funeral business and practices. One was the work of the Luthern Burial Association, working through the church, which hopes to make the funeral and burial an integral church activity in keeping with Christian tradition. The group provides a church funeral service, a simple casket (manufactured to its own specifications), a visitation in the church, and a dignified liturgical ceremony, all at a set price that not only takes care of the mortician's fee but also provides money for the church and charitable purposes. The group urges all members to take advantage of the service.

Similarly, a Reform Jewish congregation in a Chicago suburb has formed a congregational funeral committee that has arranged a standard funeral in keeping with Jewish law and tradition. All member families are urged to call the committee as soon as death takes place and let the committee take over with the funeral it has chosen.

But if you must choose the mortician, and you want a funeral home patronized by members of your religious faith, ask your clergyman or a church member to recommend a place. You know, of course, that many mortuaries are nondenominational and nonsectarian, geared to manage funerals for all faiths. Make it a point to talk to church members who recently have been through a bereavement. They can recommend a funeral director who is both supportive and ethical.

Try to make your first decision the final one. As soon as you call a funeral home, someone will come to pick up the body (particularly if it is at a convalescent or nursing home). Once the body is in the mortuary, it may be difficult, and expensive, to transfer it to a second home you have decided upon after more deliberate thought. Persuasive efforts will be made to convince you not to do so; at this time you hardly need any additional pressures.

If you are concerned about the costs of funeral and burial, talk with someone who knows about them from personal experience, not just through hearsay or by reading best-sellers on the high cost of death. Your clergyman, who has often accompanied parishioners to arrange a funeral for someone in the family, is a good resource, as are friends who recently experienced a death in the family and have gone through what you must go through now.

It's important to get the facts about what the costs in your community really are. Most people have a very unrealistic idea of what funerals and cemetery lots cost. Sociologist Robert Fulton found in a survey conducted in the 1960s that over three-fourths of the general public had no idea at all of the average price for a funeral in their own community. The percentage may have improved in the past five years, but ignorance of prevailing prices is still very high.

While it's true that you need not judge what you want in a funeral by its price tag alone, by the same token you shouldn't have to pay extra or inflated prices if you *are* concerned about price.

Listen to what appears to you to be the most knowledgeable opinion—and then call the mortician who will either come out immediately to pick up the body, or else ask you to come to the funeral home for a consultation. There you make the arrangements and pick out the casket.

Details of what will take place at this conference are discussed in a later chapter.

14

The Sudden Accidental Death:
Immediate Steps

What to do in the case of a sudden, unexpected death is quite different from the procedure that takes place when death is expected. In the latter, you are prepared to some degree to what is going to happen, and when it does, the institutional personnel are there to give you support. In the case of sudden death, you are totally on your own.

DEATH IN THE HOME

You're at home, the two of you. Suddenly there's a terrible fall from the roof where your spouse was fixing the television antenna. Or you find a still body in bed after a too-long nap. Or a car comes speeding into the driveway where your spouse is working. You take one look: and you know he's dead! What do you do?

The most important thing to do is to confirm that death actually has taken place. Call the professionals. Immediately call the fire department or the paramedics (if they operate in your community) to give immediate, life-saving first aid. If you don't know the direct number to call, dial 911 (where that emergency number is in use) or "O" for Operator. Tell whomever answers that you need immediate help, and give your address as clearly as you can.

One Los Angeles physician feels this step is vital. "I always tell people: Call the paramedics *first*. I can't possibly get there as fast as they can; they use a siren which I don't have. In fact, I insist they *always* call the paramedics. I *never* trust the family's judgment on death. We've seen too many patients that the family diagnosed as dead who really were alive."

As soon as you can, call your family physician, if you have one. If someone in your family has been seeing one recently, you will have that number close at hand.

Tell the doctor what happened. He or she will either come right over, or will question you on the phone to get more details, perhaps suggesting the fire department resuscitation unit call back as soon as they are finished.

If the paramedics cannot revive the person, they still may want to take the body to the emergency room at the hospital for further measures. Go along and talk to the doctors there.

Don't be alarmed when the police also show up at the house. Usually a call to the fire department automatically alerts the police switchboard. The police will stay until the person is removed to the emergency hospital or the resuscitation unit indicates there is no hope.

Unless it is an obviously accidental death, the police officers will ask you if there has been a medical history. If so, they'll call your physician (if the doctor isn't there already), who will be asked to sign the death certificate. A doctor who has seen the patient within a limited number of days before the death occurred (and this number varies from state to state) and is willing to certify that the cause of death was natural, will agree to sign the death certificate. In that case, the police will suggest you call a mortuary and will stay with you until things get under control. But if the physician can't certify the cause of death, then the unexpected death is ruled "a coroner's case," requiring a special type of investigation.

Coroner's cases involve one basic factor: sudden, unexpected death. A special investigation for such cases is a peculiarly Anglo-Saxon institution, virtually unknown in continental Europe except where there is manifest evidence of foul play. While the coroner's procedures in the United States may vary from jurisdiction to jurisdiction, by and large the philosophy, *modus operandi,* and objectives are the same everywhere.

Whenever a sudden, unexpected death takes place, a county official, usually the county coroner or medical examiner, is legally responsible for finding out the cause of death. (In the states that don't have coroners or medical examiners, the county official has a different title.)

Any case in which the person's physician was not in immediate attendance is a coroner's case. What constitutes "immediate attendance" varies from state to state. In Illinois the deceased must have been attended by a licensed physician (in person, not just by telephone) sometime in the previous seventy-two hours. In California it must have been within the previous twenty days. Other states have other limits. In the experience of most people, the death in the family that becomes a coroner's case is a death by accident or the sudden death of persons presumably in good health.

If the police are at the home already, they themselves call the coroner's office. If not the police, your physician will, or the fire department, or anyone else who knows of or sees the death, including yourself. The police officer then waits until the coroner's investigator arrives.

If your doctor is with you, he'll comfort you as best he

can. He might want to administer a sedative before he leaves.

But you need all the human comfort and support you can get. Call someone to be with you and your family: a relative, friend, your clergyman, or your neighbor. You must certainly have someone else there if there are any children. This includes not only little children, but even preteens and teenagers who look and act as though they are in control, but actually may be terrified. You'll never need friends' support and comfort more.

The reality of what has happened may not register all at once. You are in shock, nonetheless; and in this condition, your response may be one of many, all unusual. You may find yourself numbed, unable to do any of the things you know you must do. Or you'll find yourself responding automatically with an apparent strength and presence of mind you don't really possess. You may even become hysterical, or faint, or even begin to shake with uncontrollable laughter.

Your response will have a profound effect on the children. They will not only be frightened by the sight of the death itself, but they will be terrified by your reaction and that of the other adults around them. They will see people who all their lives have behaved predictably now suddenly behaving in impossible-to-conceive ways: crying, shaking, losing control completely. Understand that this is nothing you must apologize for or even try to hide: You're in the throes of a shock that's not of your making. But the children must have someone close at hand to reassure them that the condition of the adults around them is just temporary, that you who have always been so much in control have not gone completely berserk—for so it may appear to their frightened eyes.

Legally the body is not to be touched by anyone until the coroner's deputy arrives. According to an investigator in the Los Angeles County Coroner's office, sometimes people do disobey this injunction under the stress of the moment: The baby is picked up and put back in the crib, or a pillow is put under the mother's head. And when it's obvious that what has been done involved no criminal intent, they might ignore the violation. But it should be emphasized that the circumstances determine the culpability of such actions. If it seems a terrible strain to refrain from touching the one you loved, remember that the body is beyond any comforting action you can offer now. For your own sake it's best to obey the law.

The two investigators, one from the city or county police department and the other from the county coroner's office, will be as nonbelligerent as possible. But they have official duties to carry out, and this they will have to do.

Don't vent your anger and grief over the sudden death on these people. (It's not an infrequent occurrence according to coroner's deputies.) Try to remember that they're not responsible for the death; they are only there because the death has already occurred.

Whatever the investigator asks for is required for a report, so cooperate as much as possible. Investigators insist that often the need to concentrate on answering their questions helps survivors in this initial period of shock. The questions must be answered in any event, sooner or later.

Besides a uniformed policeman, a police detective often arrives also. Some departments automatically send a detective to the scene of a home accident and this shouldn't cause alarm.

The coroner's deputy—the one who officially conducts the investigation—is the one officer who *must* be on the scene of the accidental death. Often, the investigation simply consists of asking you questions in order to make out the death certificate. In general they are the same as must be asked in the case of an expected death.

It probably is helpful to know what kind of information is needed for the death certificate and the reasons why, so you don't feel that asking such personal questions is a malevolent intrusion on your privacy. The questions may differ somewhat in various jurisdictions, but most death certificates require the following: the name of the deceased, sex, date of death or date body was found; race, age or approximation, date of birth if known, place of death or "found at" (all for statistical purposes); the birthplace of the deceased (for statistical or genealogical purposes), place of citizenship (consular offices of various nations must be informed of the death of one of their citizens), marital status (for further identification), and name of surviving spouse (to determine eligibility for survivors' benefits, eligibility to marry, or transfer of stocks and bonds); social security number (for claimants and agencies involved in dependents' benefits), occupation (for statistics), veteran status (for claims involving dependents' benefits and statistics); residence of deceased (for statistics), parents of deceased: father's and mother's names (for identification and genealogical purposes).

Other information on the death certificate will also include the method of bodily disposition, name and address of cemetery or crematory, and name and address of the funeral home. This is filled in later.

The coroner's deputy will then have the body taken to the county morgue or a designated funeral home or hospital. It will be taken there whether you are present during the investigation or not, or whether you give permission or not. Here the official autopsy is performed.

Most accidental deaths are autopsied to certify the exact cause of death. If there is a religious aversion to an immediate autopsy, then the coroner must make note of the objection for the record. Coroners sometimes may forgo the autopsy at their discretion, as, for example, when persons die by natural causes but their religion forbids the attendance of a licensed physician (e.g., Christian Scientists). In such cases the coroner, as medical examiner, signs the death certificate forthwith. However, the coroner who feels an autopsy is necessary is legally bound to have one performed.

The coroner as medical examiner or a physician designated by the coroner performs the autopsy. How much time is allowed before the body is released for burial varies by jurisdiction. When the autopsy is completed, you, the survivor, will be notified that the body is ready to be picked up for the funeral.

Sometimes the body can be released not only to the decedent's next of kin but also to "their personal representatives, friends, or to the person designated in writing by the decedent, or to the funeral director selected by such persons," depending on the exact wording of the state statute. (In some states the looseness of the statute has led to the illegal release of bodies to so-called "friends," for removal to an unauthorized funeral home which then persuades the survivors to permit them to keep the body and conduct the funeral.)

If prior arrangements have been made to donate the body to a medical facility, you must double-check with the medical school. The case of accidental death is somewhat different from the case of the expected death. Many schools will not accept a body if an autopsy has been performed. Or if parts of the body were to be donated, not only may the autopsy be a bar, but the time that has necessarily elapsed may make the tissue unusable for transplantation. In either case, you must then call a mortuary instead and have them follow the customary procedure.

If you don't know which funeral home to call, make sure you ask only those whom you know and in whose judgment you have confidence, such as friends, relatives, perhaps your physician, perhaps even an attorney, for the name of one.

Don't ask for, or accept, the advice of casual strangers. At this point your discernment and alertness are not very great, and you are vulnerable to confidence games of all kinds. Police records show that the victims are not necessarily only the unsophisticated or the poor.

If the person died in the emergency room of a large, impersonal hospital, you may be approached by a friendly orderly or attendant, or another "survivor" in the waiting room who is only too happy to suggest a "very good, convenient" funeral home. Be wary. What you don't know is that the good Samaritan may be a "steerer" who is collecting an illegal kickback from a funeral home for every body sent there. You can be sure that the funeral director there will treat you as an easy and legitimate mark for all the expensive trappings that can be loaded on you. Or you might be overcharged for normal, or minimal, service. Regular hospital personnel or people connected with the police department or coroner's office are not allowed to make direct recommendations or suggestions.

DEATH AWAY FROM HOME

If the accidental or sudden death took place while you were at work or shopping, or if it happened in another city, part of the above sequence is altered, depending on where you were located and how soon you were told of the death.

You most certainly will be notified in person: not by phone, not by telegram. All police forces and coroner's officers throughout the country are advised to follow this procedure, although of course there may be exceptions where through negligence or simply lack of personnel it won't be done. Not only is it more humane this way, but sometimes the shock to the survivor after hearing about the death requires that someone be right there in case of medical repercussions. If the police can't do it, they try to have someone even closer to you break the news, perhaps your supervisor at work.

If the accident took place away from home, it's most likely the body will have been removed by the time you reach the scene. But the person who notified you should have other information about where the body is or a number to call. The phone number may be the police station where the investigating officer is stationed, or the morgue, or the name of the emergency hospital where the victim was pronounced dead.

The subsequent period, from the time you learn of the death until you see the body again in the mortuary of your choice, may be the most harrowing part of the experience. This will be particularly true if the death took place out of town.

What you want to know most of all at this point is what happened: Who saw the accident, did your loved one suffer, what was done with the body, can you see it, when can you bring the body back home? The answers to these questions seem simple enough—but sometimes you may feel people on the other end act as though it's classified information.

Try to remember that the death is terribly important to you, but in all probability it's just part of the routine duties of those associated with the body and the accident. There will be delays in reaching people who can give you accurate information. Sometimes those you talk to have no information at all, or you're told the records are in transit and no one is around to locate them at this time, or no one answers at all at the phone number you were given.

Your only recourse is to persist. Call the twenty-four–hour number of the police department or the coroner's office in the jurisdiction where the death took place. Explain to whomever you talk to what you want to find out; perhaps the person on the other end can suggest whom else to check with. If it's late at night, ask the person to check the records and call you back. If you don't hear in a few hours call back again.

You may have to make many phone calls, and in your grief and frustration panic may set in. You may become so upset you become incoherent, or in your anger lose all patience and find it impossible to get even the minimum of cooperation.

At some point stop and have someone else take over for you. Somewhere out there someone exists who can give you the facts you want to know. If it's helpful at all—and it probably isn't—remember that the death has already occurred. None of the chaos, confusion, and obstruction now going on can be of concern to the one you loved. It's just a part of how things work in the here and now, infinitely more abrasive because of your raw sensibilities.

Eventually it will turn out that that malevolent monster of vindictive unconcern on the other end of the telephone is just a sleepy clerk waiting to go off duty, or a coroner's deputy who had a date that evening and is stuck working overtime to clear up the paper work of this accident, or a funeral home attendant who just came on duty and hasn't been told anything. Eventually you will get the story of what happened and be satisfied that you know all there is to be told.

While the body is waiting or undergoing the autopsy, use this time to contact a funeral director. If the death happened out of town, the funeral director you contact in your town makes the arrangements with a mortician in the other city to return the body. In some jurisdictions you may be asked to go there to identify the body, particularly if an accident raised the question of correct identification. However, this is no longer routinely done. It seldom is done if the death takes place in the city in which you live. Identification is almost always made by some other means, such as checking the contents of the wallet or purse for a driver's license or tracing other relevant material. Even in cases of disasters, identification clues as birthmarks, operation scars, or dental charts are preferred to eye identification by the next of kin.

You, on the other hand, may *want* to see the body in the morgue before it's released to the funeral home. Ask to do so if you wish, but it's a privilege given at the coroner's discretion.

If you are told to come down to see the body, remember that in counties covering a large physical area what is called "the county morgue" is not necessarily a single building in the downtown area of the county seat. It may be a number of county facilities scattered over the county, or one or more hospitals, or even designated funeral homes chosen as repositories for coroner's cases. Therefore, if you're going to the county morgue make sure you know the exact address of the building where the body is.

Sometimes a designated funeral home will try to persuade you to allow it to keep the body and arrange the subsequent funeral. You're under no obligation to do this if you have another funeral home in mind (or even if you decide to use another one but haven't a name at the moment). Simply ask the funeral home you eventually choose to pick up the body. There will be legitimate charges the first funeral home may make for services already performed (such as transportation, preparation, and embalming); in many cases, the amount is set by law. These may or may not be paid by the second funeral home as included in their services.

DEATH IN ANOTHER COUNTRY

One very special instance of sudden, unexpected death that must be treated here is what to do if your spouse, parent, or friend dies while on vacation or on a business trip in another country.

If death should take place while you're along on the trip,

notify the local authorities immediately. Then without delay, *at once*, contact the closest American embassy or consulate in the country in which you find yourself. Tell them what happened and ask for immediate assistance.

This is essential for a number of reasons. The local medical and legal requirements that must be fulfilled when death takes place vary widely from locale to locale, and only the consular officer is thoroughly familiar with the customs of that particular place. Yet being an American, the officer understands and is sympathetic to your wishes to follow American customs and procedures and will try to see that your wishes are followed, consistent with the requirements of the country in which you are traveling. Finally, the consular official is the one who can handle what has to be done as quickly and effortlessly as possible; this is not an infrequent occurrence in consulates around the world and the person who takes charge probably has handled this sort of thing many times before.

Your big problem is the first step, making contact with the United States consulate.

In industrialized countries with a fairly sophisticated urban culture and a fairly efficient telephone system, you will have the least amount of difficulty, particularly where people speak English and Americans are familiar and accepted tourists. Either the people at the hotel where you are staying or the public officials will easily put you in touch with the embassy or the local consulate. (There is only one embassy building in each country with which we have diplomatic relations, usually in the capital city. But if the country is large or highly industrialized, there are also U.S. consulates in other principal cities.)

Your problems increase as you travel to parts of the world where English is not a familiar language, where telephone systems and efficiency are poor, or where local authorities are comparatively autonomous and may be hostile to any suggestion that their normal method of procedure may not be suitable in this instance.

In such cases, when you do not speak the language, a good local interpreter is imperative, not only one who speaks both English and the local language, but who can work with local authorities, translating your needs in their terms. A local American resident or an English-speaking local living there may be your best contact. If such a person cannot be located, then the hotel manager, a police official, even a willing by-stander must be relied upon.

Often, and unfortunately, time is crucial since there may be no way the body can be preserved if negotiations are pro-tracted or if the local health officer or police cannot be con-tacted readily. You must persist in insisting that the embassy or consulate be contacted, for the officials there are the only ones who can take care of your interests and requirements.

Should you get someone to help you, by all means offer to pay him or her for services rendered. The persons who help you may refuse to take your money; this is their prerog-ative. But do not presume that they will help you out of the goodness of their hearts. Even if they do nothing more than contact the U.S. authorities for you, the work they must do may be difficult and time-consuming. Understand that it also may be costly; they may have to offer gratuities all along the line to cut red tape and get action going.

Once you get in touch with the American consular officer, your problems will be considerably eased. The consular officer can tell you what can be done with the body, for example, or if an autopsy is required. He or she can tell you if em-balming is possible so the body can be shipped home. (In some countries, embalming is unheard of; in others, it is diffi-cult and expensive to obtain; in still others, it is relatively common and inexpensive.) The officer can also tell you what other alternatives for disposing of the body exist: burial in the country where the death took place (in some countries with a large expatriate American population, there are American sections in the local cemetery), shipment of the unembalmed body back to the United States in a sealed casket, or cremation in the country and shipment of the ashes back home.

Since money may be crucial—particularly if no arrangements had been made previously for ready cash in such an unforeseen contingency—the consulate will assist you in getting in touch with your bank, your lawyer, or relatives in the United States so that you can get cash to meet all needs. (They may even advance you the money if the need is immediate and urgent.)

The consulate official can give you an estimate of the relative costs of the various alternatives and the time all the processing may take, particularly if a local autopsy is required before a final death certificate is issued.

Finally, and this is vital, the officer will see to it that you get all the final papers required as legal proof of the death so that when you return home you can claim insurance, settle the estate, and close out whatever legal matters remain that depend on certifying that the death occurred.

If death of your spouse, parent, or friend occurs while you are with a tour group, then the tour guide will assume responsibility for getting in touch with the American consulate and will assist you in every way to get all the necessary matters taken care of.

Last of all, if you are *not* on the trip, then the State Department will get in touch with you at home. The official will explain to you how the death took place, and then will proceed according to your wishes. You may wish to go to the country where it happened and escort the body back (although this is not necessary). Or you may choose one of various alternatives. If you choose to have the body shipped back to the United States, you will be asked the name of the mortuary to which the body is to be shipped. You will also be told approximately when the casket can be expected so you'll know when the funeral can be scheduled. The State Department officer will help you in every way to ease the shock of the sudden, unexpected death.

The next step, the arrangement for the funeral and burial, is considered in another chapter.

15

The Suicide and the Homicide:
Immediate Steps

Most coroner's cases for the next of kin are, as mentioned, death by accident or the unexpected, sudden death of someone presumably in good health. But coroner's cases also include suicides and homicides.

Of the 1,933,000 deaths that took place in America in 1974, both natural and sudden, unexpected ones, 47,210 were classified as suicides or homicides. And despite the fact that these deaths are comparatively rare occurrences, their incidence is distributed unevenly among cities of varying sizes, among the various racial, ethnic, or age groupings, and in the different parts of the country. They may happen in your family.

Suicide and homicide have a special aura of horror about them that intensifies all our negative feelings about death, adding a new dimension to the trauma. The act of self-destruction throws a tremendous burden of guilt upon the family that remains. And when someone in the family is murdered, we feel tainted in a particularly ugly way, often suffused with a burning shame, for no accountable reason.

In both instances, a new stress is added to the heightened tension: the active and not necessarily supportive intervention of the police.

But stripped of its subjective aura, the procedure in case of suicide or homicide is not much different than what takes place when the death is by accident.

SUICIDE

If you find the suicide's body and there is no question that the person is dead, call the police immediately. The police will call the coroner. Then do not, repeat, *do not touch or move anything* before the police get there.

This must be borne in mind particularly when suicide takes place. The social and religious stigma attached to suicide makes everyone involved fervently wish that the death had been accidental and not self-inflicted. It is the wish to avoid the condemnation of friends and the community at large, far more than the financial motive for insurance money that might be withheld from the beneficiaries, that prompts some people to try to make the death appear accidental.

Police and coroner's investigators have innumerable stories of such attempts. While admitting that there may be cases where such deceptions are successful, they are very skeptical whether nonprofessionals can ever pull it off, particularly since suicide cases trigger very intensive investigations. Tampering with evidence is clearly and unquestionably illegal, subjecting those who do it to criminal prosecution. This additional burden is one you surely do not need.

The trauma of confronting death under such frightening circumstances is much greater than the accidental death, and much more so than when death is expected. Psychologist Robert Kavanaugh describes the acute shock as though "the real and the unreal worlds clash in collision. The bodily systems gallop while the mind reels in conflict, hearing and rejecting, knowing and blocking, plus a host of individual reactions. Fainting . . . hysterical laughter . . . uncontrollable behavior. . . ."

Call someone immediately while you can, to stay with you: someone you can talk to, scream at, cry with, hold on to.

The trauma of a suicide in the close family is particularly demolishing to children. For preteenagers the act is perhaps even more incomprehensible than homicide. While they can accept the idea of someone being killed by another, their own ego systems are so central to their beings that the idea of self-destruction creates earthshaking panic. Make absolutely sure someone is with them always, someone as receptive, as compassionate as possible—but not a total stranger, and not someone who will whisk them away to an institution or even out of the city (although they should never be permitted to remain in the presence of the body).

It is not necessarily bad if the person who cares for the children is also affected by the death—the very act of mutually consoling each other (although the child receives more than he gives) may help the child eventually to grasp that the death was not personally aimed at him or her but was a universal tragedy.

Having someone always with a child is even more necessary if it's a male teenager. They as a class are particularly vulnerable as potential suicides, and they need special and very perceptive support.

You yourself may need not only nonprofessional support but professional medical help. Call your doctor if you have a health history yourself which may be aggravated under this high stress. Also call your lawyer, if you have one, to act as a friendly adviser, simply because in your state the fear of questioning by the police is very great, even if you are completely divorced from what happened.

Understand that you are going to be asked all kinds of questions by the police investigators. This is their duty. They are not totally callous to your suffering; they probably have made no personal judgment at all about you or the one who is dead.

What happens is just the unfortunate by-product of their profession and your own vulnerability: Their behavior may appear to you to be totally insensitive. To them, there is a job to be finished as quickly as possible. As professionals they've been in similar situations time and time again, and they have questioned many people just as upset as you. They justify their bluntness and insistence on detail by asserting that on the basis of their extensive experience the need to answer their specific, hard questions helps calm survivors, concentrating their thoughts away from the horror of death, distracting them despite themselves.

The first officer who arrives usually has the job of protecting the area around the body, so you will be asked to go to some other part of the house. If the death took place out in the open, the police will ask you to sit in the squad car. Insist if you wish on having some friend be with you at all times, if only to hold your hand. The uniformed officer may ask some preliminary questions or may wait until the detectives or coroner's investigators come to question you.

You'll certainly be asked to tell what you can about the death—and there may be other questions as well. While they're talking to you other officers will be photographing the scene and doing what they must about checking the body. This should take place out of your sight. Eventually the body will be removed and taken to the morgue for an autopsy. After the autopsy is completed, you will be notified to request your mortuary to remove the body for the funeral.

At some time after the autopsy takes place, if the coroner feels the facts warrant it, an inquest may be held. This is a public hearing to establish the mode of death. It probably will be held after the funeral and burial are over—and to you it may seem utterly uncalled for, considering the strain the family is under.

But according to coroner's investigators this is required by law, because sometimes the facts are not as self-evident as you feel they are. Since the payment of considerable insurance may rest on the question, it is essential to establish how the person did, in fact, meet death. It certainly must be established if it was by deliberate intent.

Often there are a number of possible causes of death, some natural and others deliberate. Did the person who took an overdose of barbiturates actually die of the drug? Or was the person only in a coma when a cigarette set fire to the house, and the actual cause of death was smoke inhalation?

Although it seems a terrible invasion of human privacy and decency to rake the whole episode over again in the glare of public inquiry, the process is a necessary one and not intended for harassment.

HOMICIDE

The treatment of a homicide is in general the same as the previous instances of accidental death. In this case society's interest in the crime intrudes the police even more into your life. If you discover the body, call the police; then absolutely do not, repeat, *absolutely do not touch or disturb anything* around the body, in the room, or elsewhere that may have anything to do with the crime.

Now, more than ever, you should have someone with you.

Besides friends, have your doctor there in case your health requires that you be excused from extensive questioning or in case you need a sedative as a cushion against the shock.

Besides the uniformed police officers, the homicide detectives, specialists from the technical branches of the crime laboratory, and the coroner's investigator will be there. There will be much turmoil and the police will take you aside for questioning, even if you are not regarded by them as a suspect. You will not be permitted to sit near the dead body or grieve at the scene; the area around the homicide will be closed off to everyone except the professionals who must work there.

At this point, according to the Los Angeles coroner's deputies, questioning is less of an interrogation than a need for information. When did you see the person alive? What happened when you discovered the body? Did the victim have any enemies? Were there any threats? Sometimes you will be asked to come to the station, usually simply to get away from the scene.

After they've talked to you, the police may suggest that you go and stay temporarily with a relative, friend, or neighbor until they finish working on the premises, remove the body, and clean up. Sometimes, however, the scene of the crime must be put under lock and key for quite a while, possibly until the entire investigation is over. In that case, you will be asked to make more permanent living arrangements until your house or apartment is available for you to return.

If you feel you may be suspect or be implicated in the crime, get in touch with a lawyer—who will stay at your side when the police question you—as soon as you have called the police. Make sure it is an attorney who specializes in criminal law and not just a friend. As an amateur pitted against professionals who are working in their familiar territory, you should have all the professional help you can get. You do not know your rights or the intricacies of the law; an attorney does.

After their preliminary questioning the police have a right to ask you to go down to the police station for further interrogation. Cooperate as you wish, on the advice of your attorney and physician. If the police feel they have reason to do so, they may detain you for a limited time. After that they must officially charge you with a crime or release you.

The body will be taken down to the morgue and treated as in the case of an accidental death, except that the autopsy may take more time. After the autopsy is completed and various tissues or wound areas are removed, the body will be released to the funeral home of your choice. Now, as with the natural and the sudden, accidental death, you deal with the funeral director to arrange the final rites.

16

Making Arrangements for the Funeral and Burial

It's understandable that you have strong feelings of unease and suspicions about going to see the mortician, and not only because you are making the death arrangements, which in themselves are unsettling. There has been such an outcry by both responsible government agencies and public interest groups (as well as individuals) about the strong likelihood that you will be subjected to excessive cost and misrepresentation of goods and services that you are naturally apprehensive. In addition, since you *must* buy what the mortician is selling, you know you're not in a very good bargaining position.

To protect yourself you may be tempted to follow the advice of all critics of the funeral industry and, surprisingly enough, the advice of a spokesman for the industry as well, to take someone with you, particularly one who will not be panicked (as you are told you will be) into making over-extended purchases and unwise commitments.

Many people who have actually had extensive experience dealing with morticians in just such a role feel the fear has been exaggerated.

Professor Robert Kavanaugh, former priest and now teacher of psychology, who frequently was asked by others to visit the mortician with them, found the results less than satisfactory. "When asked to accompany grievers or when volunteering, I felt a need to be protective, almost a hero, sometimes preventing grievers from splurging a bit to fulfill their deepest needs. Whether I like it or not, expensive funerals are one way the economically oriented have for relieving some guilt. Afterwards my role was sometimes resented, my decisions questioned, and all mistakes were laid on me. Neither funeral director nor family was happy, nor was I."

His advice is to find the ethical funeral director *before* you go, one whom others recommend as a person in whom they have confidence. Then go to the mortuary with a relative or friend for support, but not necessarily "to protect you." You can assume (until you have reason to believe otherwise) that the interest of the funeral director is not much different from your own.

A recent public television program on death aired in Chicago confirmed this view when it presented a number of morticians who appeared ethical, compassionate, and understanding. Kavanaugh's advice is in line with these findings. "With a truly professional funeral director . . . no fear of being robbed or misled need affect an already overburdened mind. He will do whatever grievers truly want and will take time to find out their desires."

Remember there are already both local and state laws operating now (some enforced better than others) which circumscribe funeral directors' actions. They are keenly aware of them, even if you are not.

What follows is a general idea of what will take place in the interview, although not applicable everywhere. The events will not necessarily happen in this order.

CONFERRING WITH THE FUNERAL DIRECTOR

The conference with the funeral director should take place while the body is still at the hospital, although it may have already been removed at your request to the mortuary. The Federal Trade Commission in August 1975 came out with a proposed trade regulation for funeral homes, and one of its recommendations was that funeral homes not be permitted to pick up the body without prior consent of the family. This is to prevent, among other things, the various confidence games played on survivors, as mentioned in previous chapters.

After the funeral director has put you at your ease, there may be some general discussion preceding more specific arrangements for the funeral and burial. Since the funeral director is the person who fills in the death certificate details, although the attending physician signs it, he or she must get certain information for the death certificate; this has already been enumerated in an earlier chapter. Some questions can be answered from the hospital records when the body is picked up, but the rest must be asked of you. Some of them sound very personal and unnecessary, but the answers are legally required.

Then the mortician will discuss the funeral with you, presumably in a comforting, nonaggressive way. There are a number of large decisions, some of which you have already made. Others may seem like small details but are still necessary. By all means ask the mortician's opinion or for an explanation of your alternatives as you go along.

You must decide if the body is to be buried, entombed, or cremated. In connection with the first and last, if there is any deviation from normal funeral practice (such as having an immediate burial or cremation without viewing), make certain the mortician knows of it at once, particularly if embalming is to be eliminated. The embalming may already have been done if you had not requested otherwise when you gave directions to pick up the body; it's ordinarily done as a routine matter unless the mortician is notified beforehand. But if the body is still in the hospital or the morgue, your request should be complied with. It's hoped the mortician will also make a downward adjustment on your final bill as well. (The proposed FTC regulation would prohibit embalming without the oral consent of the next of kin and would require a monetary adjustment.)

If you want the body cremated, you must tell the mortician whether it will be immediate cremation or a cremation after open-casket viewing. If it's without viewing, you'll presumably want an inexpensive container rather than an expensive casket. The right to request this is also a part of the FTC recommendation, and the mortician should honor your request. (Only two states, Massachusetts and Michigan, actually require caskets if the body is to be cremated.)

If there is viewing, the funeral director will want to know for how many days, what hours, and whether it will be in the funeral home or the church. At the same time you must also set the date and hour for the funeral itself—and again stipulate whether it will be in the funeral home or the church, and whether the casket is to be opened or closed during the religious ceremony.

If the body is to be buried, a cemetery lot must be bought. If it will be entombed, you must have a crypt. If the cremated remains are to be put in an urn, you must get a niche at a columbarium.

The funeral director usually does not sell cemetery property unless the home is part of a mortuary-cemetery dual operation. He or she may get a plot for you—or may be forbidden to do so—depending on the state and the prevailing custom. But the director certainly will be conversant on cemetery plot or crypt prices and can tell you how they vary among the local cemeteries. If you wish, an appointment can be made for you with someone at the place you choose, after you are finished in the funeral home.

If your spouse is a veteran and you'd like him buried in a veterans cemetery (perhaps intending to be buried there yourself), the funeral director will get in touch with the closest Veterans Administration office for you and find out where the nearest veterans cemetery is that is still open for burials. The closest one may not be nearby; it may even be in an adjoining state. However, if you still wish the body buried there, arrange with the funeral director either to have it embalmed and shipped by common carrier or put in a casket and driven out by hearse. The cost of the transportation may be high, but the fact that the burial and grave marker are free offsets the cost.

Tell the funeral director which clergyman, if any, will preside, and decide between you who should contact him.

Then there are the smaller details: the flowers, what clothes the body will be buried in, who the pallbearers should be, how many funeral cars are to be in the cortege to the cemetery, what kind of music, whether a fraternal lodge's ceremony is to be included, and so forth. An obituary will have to be written, so the funeral director will ask personal questions about the one who died, and ask the names and occupations of the survivors. This is the time to suggest, if you wish, a memorial fund to which friends can contribute in lieu of flowers; the notice ordinarily appears in the obituary. You may also be asked at this time how many certified copies of the death certificate you'll need (for insurance purposes, or to transfer property).

The funeral director will do as much, or as little, as you ask; but of course you will be charged for anything over the amount that is part of the normal service. It is up to you to decide what you want done—and what you, your friends, and relatives want to do for yourselves. Some people are so distraught they would just as soon have the mortician take care of everything: choosing the minister, the music, the floral arrangements, the pallbearers, even notifying the relatives out of town and friends. Such people feel that, no matter how much extra it costs, they would just as soon not have to concern themselves with these minutiae.

But one essential thing you must do is choose the casket. Choosing the casket is surrounded with a mystique all its own, a bright penumbra of anxieties, doubts, and secret expectations. Among other reasons for anxiety, it is certainly the most costly piece of merchandise you have to buy at this time.

The cost of the casket is part of the entire package of goods and services called the standard adult funeral. Exactly what in the package is casket and what constitutes service and facilities is a little fuzzy. The recent FTC-proposed regulation would permit this practice for funerals only below a certain minimum. With all others, the price of the casket must be segregated from the facilities and services, and an itemized list of all merchandise and services selected, together with a statement about the variety, cost, and arrangement of caskets in the display room (including deletion for services or goods not requested) is to be signed as having been read before you enter the display room.

After the funeral director explains the details (possibly not as fully as the recommended ruling suggests), you will be taken into a display room where anywhere from twelve to thirty different caskets in varying price ranges, colors, privileged positions of display, and degrees of lavishness can be seen (and not necessarily in neat order from the least to the most expensive). You may be allowed to look them over by yourself or the director may walk around with you and answer any questions or volunteer information that you may request.

Above each casket is usually a price card. Again, at one time this was invariably the price of the standard adult funeral. Already this single-unit method of pricing has given way in many states to a more elaborate breakdown of charges. Very often the price of the casket will be listed separate from the remaining charges.

You must always keep in mind as you look over the caskets (although the funeral director may not necessarily remind you) that the cost of the standard adult funeral is just a fraction, though a large fraction, of the total cost that you're going to have to pay. Frequently people have a particular money figure in mind to spend (say, $1000), and then are pleasingly surprised to find the cost of the funeral and casket falls comfortably within that figure. But there are other costs you must remember, and they are important.

First, there are the "extras" that the funeral home will charge that are not included in the package, although these may already have been delineated on the itemized statement you've seen before going into the display room. They include the burial clothing, extra limousines, special costs for special requests or for special displays. There are also the out-of-pocket advances the mortician makes to others, which you will be charged for: money to the florist for the flowers you requested, the honorarium to the clergyman you've selected, the obituary to the newspapers (which, surprisingly, charge for this service), and other items. You should only be charged for true out-of-pocket expenses and not for extra profit, as the FTC found has happened frequently.

Then there are the substantial costs at the cemetery: the cemetery lot (if you have not yet purchased one) or the mausoleum crypt or niche in the columbarium. There is the cost of the burial vault (if not purchased from the funeral home: another "extra"), and the opening and closing costs for the grave. Also you must keep in mind the cost of the memorial stone and the additional charge of having it installed.

Meaningful figures as to how much these additional costs add to the original figure of the standard adult funeral are hard to get, not only from industry sources but from investigative agencies and groups as well. The National Funeral Directors Association has estimated that the standard adult funeral is about 77 percent of the total funeral home costs. Adding to this the cemetery charges and the gravestone costs, it is realistic for you mentally to add another half again to the cost of the standard adult funeral in order to get a realistic cost figure for the total funeral and burial package.

The real difficulty you will have making up your mind about what you want to spend on the funeral may not come from any pressure from the funeral director but from your own ambivalent, not well-understood feelings. On one hand you want to do the right thing for the one you loved. Yet you don't want to squander money that you'll need to take care of your future and those of your dependents. In the end, without knowing how it happened, any original resolve you have in holding to a particular figure may give way. All the charges seem to add up so quickly that, in order to have a certain elegance in both casket and funeral, you may spend more (sometimes a lot more) than you originally thought you would.

Psychologists and sociologists have many explanations for what seems to be a rather consistent tendency to overspend rather than underspend on the funeral and burial. Documented findings seem to point to the fact that unconscious, irrational motives influence our decisions just as surely as rational, sensible reasons; and both occur in people who are normally in good psychological health.

Whatever your reasons for doing what you want to do, now is not the time to castigate yourself. Do what seems right at the moment and be done with it. Since you cannot choose *not* to deal with the mortician, obviously your bargaining position is poor. Your only plan of action must be to ask the funeral director for the kind of casket and services you want—and then ask that the cost be adjusted accordingly, if adjustment is due. (If your state has protective laws requiring this, it helps to know it and say so.)

The matter of how all these costs are to be paid for will be discussed in the next chapter.

THE CEMETERY LOT

When you go to buy the cemetery lot, you may choose a cemetery devoted solely to members of your religious faith or choose to go to a nonsectarian one (or a large cemetery with different sections for the different faiths).

Your choice in picking a cemetery lot is more restricted than picking a funeral director. With a funeral director, particularly a neighborhood one whose reputation is dependent on your goodwill and your family's return business, there is some built-in protection of satisfaction guaranteed. With a cemetery there is less, although this isn't meant to imply that there is widespread unethical activity here. But the first body of a family group buried in a cemetery is like a lodestone—with each additional body buried in that cemetery the pressure on the family for all to be buried there increases.

In addition, cemeteries are places, not just goods and services. They have a stability, a sense of perpetuity stretching on into the indefinite future, that exercises a subtle influence which determines and circumscribes the choice of family members in the future.

Be that as it may, you don't have much time to deliberate. You must have a plot within the next few days, one that can be prepared immediately. Unless you own a family lot or have a lot already purchased, you must pay whatever is asked at the cemetery you choose or go to another cemetery for a lot that is a better buy.

But even if your decision can't be protracted, it should be a deliberate one. If you want a double lot, you must purchase both now; if you want a double interment, you must decide now before the first body is buried. Ask about the cost of the burial vault or cement liner (if not already bought from the funeral home) and if it is required by the cemetery; also what the opening and closing charges are, how much is required for their perpetual-care endowment fund or other perpetual-care provisions, and the cost of a memorial marker or gravestone and installation charge.

Buying the gravestone is one decision you may postpone temporarily at least. Since it will have to be engraved, it can't be completed in time for the burial anyway. This will give you a little time to think about what you want written on it, if you want a single or double stone, whether you want bronze or granite, if granite what kind, and the size. These are all big decisions, hardly ones you want to make in haste or under stress.

Sadly, the time for protesting the high cost of death, if indeed it upsets you, is past as far as this particular funeral is concerned. Your only recourse, shopping around more to find a funeral home or cemetery more to your liking, is hardly practicable, although it has been done. If you feel you have a real grievance, you can seek legal redress later when this is all over. As a more sensible solution, you can prevent all this unseemly rush and pressure from happening again by doing what should have been done before: planning in advance.

17

Arranging to Pay the Funeral and Burial Costs

The matter of paying the funeral and burial costs will come up at some time during your initial interview with the funeral director and the cemetery agent. They will tell you of many sources you can draw upon, both from government and the private sector. You also have a number of options for coming up with the rest of the cash.

GOVERNMENT DEATH BENEFITS

VETERANS ADMINISTRATION

If your spouse was a veteran who served on active duty with the armed forces and received a discharge that wasn't dishonorable, you as spouse are eligible for a $250 lump-sum payment for the funeral, a free cemetery plot in a national cemetery, or, in lieu of that, $150 in cash for burial elsewhere, and a free burial marker or headstone. There are 103 national cemeteries in the United States today, sixty-two of which still have available grave space.

If your spouse died while an active or retired member of the armed forces, $800 and up is offered as a death gratuity, plus $250 for the funeral and a free burial plot.

To make claim for the veteran's lump-sum death benefit, application must be made to the VA; they will not get in touch with you. The funeral director, however, has been supplied with the official application blanks and will help you fill them out. The form requires enlistment and service information, so you must bring your spouse's discharge papers from which the funeral director can get the needed details. (Incidentally, a request for the death benefit alerts the VA insurance division, so if your spouse had any kind of GI insurance, an insurance claim form is automatically sent to you as beneficiary.)

This money is available only for funeral and burial expenses, so you probably will want to authorize the funeral director you've asked to conduct the funeral to receive the money. If you do, the VA mails the check directly to the mortician, and this amount is deducted from the amount you have left to pay.

If you are not a spouse but are assuming responsibility for the funeral, you may either pay the bill in full and the Veterans Administration will reimburse you, or pay the bill in full less that amount, and the VA will reimburse the funeral director.

SOCIAL SECURITY ADMINISTRATION

A lump-sum death benefit of $255 is also given the spouse —or anyone else who assumes responsibility for the funeral and burial—of anyone insured under social security. As with the VA, the money does not come to you automatically. But in the case of this agency, they start the proceedings on their own.

In an arrangement with most mortuaries, the SSA is notified by the mortuary when a death takes place with the submission of a 721 form, the "Statement of Death." This serves in lieu of the death certificate until the official certificate is issued. With this and another mortuary-submitted form that gives even more details on the death, the SSA person contacts you to let you know about the social security benefits you are entitled to and alerts you to what you need to make a claim. To receive the lump-sum death benefit, the only thing you need to show is that you were indeed the current spouse, living with the insured. If you are not the spouse, then other verifying documents are required to establish your right to the death-benefit money.

The SSA contact is usually by phone now; the agency has instituted a nationwide teleservice operation that appears to be handling matters very well.

The funeral director will also offer to initiate action to get the social security claim started for you. However, social security people advise against it, for two reasons. First, the SSA *will* contact you, so it is a duplication of effort. Secondly, when you apply for the lump-sum death benefit, you'll also apply for other survivors' benefits, and there may be special features about your case that only the SSA claims representative knows about and can deal with. According to one district office operations manager, funeral directors often have only limited information. Frequently they so confuse the claims issue that more time is lost than saved by relying on their help.

For the survivors of persons who didn't qualify for social security but were insured under other government programs, there are often lump-sum death benefits available that are similar to social security, but the programs vary. Since funeral directors seldom have precise information about these programs, those who are eligible must get in touch with the related offices on their own.

NONGOVERNMENT DEATH BENEFITS

ORGANIZATIONS AND CLUBS

Cash to cover funeral and burial expenses may be forthcoming from various organizations the deceased belonged to. If the fraternal organizations, lodges, and social clubs do furnish money for "burial expenses" (stemming back in history when many of the groups actually started out as burial societies), they will pay the money directly to you.

But unless you have the names and addresses to give the funeral director so he can help you apply for the funds, you'll have to collect this money on your own. Search through the papers of your spouse or parent for a list or for membership certificates of organizations to which you can write. If you don't know where to look, ask his or her close friends if they know or can find out which organizations offer a benefit to which you're entitled.

LABOR UNIONS

Some labor unions have fairly substantial death benefits for the survivors of members, as part of their pension and welfare fund programs. If the funeral director knows about these supplemental funds, he will again offer to help you make application.

However, where the money forthcoming is substantial, evidence of the unethical use of this private information has come to light. One union official in New York testified at a

Senate hearing that whenever the local funeral directors found out the amount available in death benefits (which was meant to provide postdeath money as well as cover the funeral costs), survivors always ended up with more elaborate funerals, often absorbing the exact amount of the benefit. An official of another union in Detroit, reporting the same abuse there, indicated that as a matter of policy the union *never* revealed the incidence or amount of funeral or burial coverage on members, although many funeral directors called the union office directly for this information.

MORTUARY PREPAYMENT PLANS

You have already checked through the papers of the one who died (looking for the name of a local mortuary), so you're fairly certain there was no participation in a local mortuary prepayment plan. But you may have come across either a contract or a passbook that indicates there are pre-paid funds for a funeral with an out-of-town funeral home, even one in another state. (This is more likely with a parent than a spouse, but spouses also have made funeral arrangements without telling their partners.)

Most states now have regulatory statutes that either require that such money be placed in trust, or supervise and regulate these pre-need contracts through various state agencies in order to safeguard the money paid in. If the contract was made many years ago, you must find out if the funeral home is still in business, if the money is still there, and if you are entitled to collect it. Ask your present funeral director to help you draft a letter to the funeral home with whom the account exists, enclosing a copy of the death certificate, and asking that the money be refunded to you. (You also are entitled to the interest that has accumulated in the meanwhile; and depending on how many years ago the money was deposited, this may be considerable.) Later, if you do not hear from them, you may have to write to the state agency that regulates these funds to help you get the money.

However, and this is a big however, the regulations in the various states differ widely in content and degree of enforcement. In many, the funeral home with whom the original time-payment contract was made is permitted to deduct a certain percentage of the money for administrative expenses, in some cases running as high as 25 percent. But it does no harm to try. In fact if the money appears to be substantial, perhaps you might even want to enlist the help of an attorney to recover the amount.

INSURANCE

Your spouse or parent may have purchased "burial insurance" or "industrial insurance" at some time, specifically to cover funeral and burial costs. Another type of such insurance is "funeral insurance." This is a limited, ordinary-life policy of face value from $300 to usually no more than $5,000. The name on the policy sometimes has the word *funeral* in it, which indicates what it was purchased for.

If you come across any such policy among the private papers, check to see if it has been paid up or lapsed. (But even if it looks as though it has lapsed, don't discard it; the cash value portion may have been paying premiums to keep it in force, even if perhaps at a lower face value.) Also, check out the beneficiary.

If the funeral home to whom the policy was assigned is the one that conducted the funeral, the mortician is entitled to the money according to your spouse's or parent's wishes. However, if a funeral home is named as beneficiary or is assigned the policy but was *not* the one that conducted the funeral, then ask your attorney or insurance agent how, if at all, you can claim the money. You probably can get some recompense.

If, on the other hand, you *are* named the beneficiary, then at this moment you may want to wait before assigning the proceeds to the funeral director. It may be that you'd like to apply this money to the cemetery costs or the gravestone, and pay the funeral costs from other sources.

Small Face-Value Term Insurance Policy. You may come across a small term insurance policy that looks as if it was probably purchased to pay the funeral expenses.

Again, if you are named the sole beneficiary, you may want to weigh whether or not to sign over the policy to the funeral director. It really is best to get a picture of *all* the costs of the funeral and burial. The interment costs may be so large you will want to apply this money there (since otherwise you have had to take out a bank loan to cover the cost of the cemetery lot), rather than give it to the funeral director. But the money should be reserved for either one or the other.

OTHER CASH RESOURCES

REGULAR PASSBOOK SAVINGS ACCOUNT

Your spouse or parent may have been putting money into a regular passbook savings account, informally earmarking it for funeral expenses (you surmise).

If you find such a passbook, the funds may be temporarily blocked. Eventually, however, the money will be available. Then if other funds are not sufficient to cover the costs, the money in this savings account can pay the residue, particularly if interest has been accumulating for a number of intervening years.

CASH

If you have sufficient money in your own checking account and wish to pay off the costs of the funeral and burial, and if there is no compelling reason why you should not do so, then by all means pay off the funeral director and the cemetery bills. Both social security and the Veterans Administration will then reimburse you.

MAKING "OTHER ARRANGEMENTS"

In the event that *no* money has been put aside, and there are only the social security and perhaps VA death benefits, then other arrangements must be made to pay the funeral and cemetery bills.

Whether you can do this on the installment plan or not depends on the regulations of the different states and often, unfortunately, on how affluent the particular funeral home or cemetery corporation feels you are, the degree of your bereavement, and the ethics of the seller.

Some funeral directors don't press the matter of money at all, particularly when it's obvious that there's insurance, or if a credit check or a call to the estate attorney shows that there will be enough money in the estate to cover the debt. (Funeral costs have priority over other debts against the estate.) Sometimes, in fact, the funeral director will contact the estate attorney and work out a payment schedule directly, so the funeral home can get some money without waiting through the entire probate proceedings.

In other cases the funeral director will ask that you pay

something down, that you turn over the SSA and VA benefits you have coming, and that you come to an understanding on how the rest is to be paid. Understandably, funeral homes are reluctant to extend long-range credit after the funeral has already been held, since they have nothing to repossess if the other party reneges on the contract. If they extend a time-payment contract, it is usually for a rather short period.

Other funeral directors are even less generous. They may extend credit but at high and often hidden rates that make the entire cost far more than it should be. While local and now federal truth-in-lending laws are in force, the practice is still known to exist.

And even today, in many poor communities, some morticians have been known to demand wage garnishments from friends and relatives to cover the cost of the funeral before they will consent to proceed. In such cases, where your bargaining position is very poor, you may be forced to accept what terms you can get, although borrowing money from friends or a credit union rather than being indebted to such a party seems a preferable alternative.

Cemeteries ask, for the most part, that the cemetery lot be paid for in full, and the other costs be paid for in cash within thirty or sixty days. However, large memorial parks do extend credit (with carrying charges) for short-term periods. It may be that to pay off the cemetery a loan from a credit union or bank until other funds materialize might be the best alternative you have.

Paying for the memorial stone *will* require a time-payment contract since for many this is a very expensive, major purchase, and the terms for these vary widely.

18

Actual Burial / Cremation Rites and Procedures

Once the body is entrusted to the funeral home and the conference with the funeral director and cemetery held to settle all the details, the funeral rites begin. These are a series of activities that extend over a limited period of time (which varies according to the religious faith, the customs of the community, and the individual wishes of family members). They are structured events which fall into a sequence; like a play, they have a beginning, a middle, and an end. Because many of us have had little or no experience with an actual funeral and burial, it's helpful to review what happens. The vicarious role-playing exercise may drain away some of the mystery and apprehension from the event itself.

The family is traditionally the responsible unit, and most of the decisions fall on one person in the family (who may or may not be the closest next of kin). This person in the family is the one who confers and concurs on all questions of procedure made with the funeral director and the clergyman. Most of the time the concurrence is perfunctory. The clergyman or the funeral director suggests a certain pattern and the family agrees. Sometimes, however, the person in charge takes a more forceful stand, particularly when he or she may have previously indicated disagreement with some of the prevalent practices of the mortician or of the church. The person may insist, for example, that flowers be removed from the room with the casket and placed in another room instead; or that the casket remain closed at all times; or that guests in the church be advised there will be no processional to the graveside because internment will be private; or that the clergyman omit the eulogy, permitting a close friend to give it instead.

Usually, however, close family members do not take on any deliberate decision-making or detailed organizational work of the funeral itself. At this point professionals from outside the family are called upon to handle the ceremonials and rituals that commemorate the passing of a family member from the world of the living.

The funeral director is in charge of the funeral proceedings. On the basis of experience this is the person who usually is the one most knowledgeable regarding the procedures. In addition to exclusive mortuary duties, the funeral director's job is to see that everything proceeds smoothly; and to say that the director and staff are there to expedite, manage, and organize the ritual is not to denigrate their role or belittle the importance of the activity.

The other professional is, of course, the clergyman. Because over 90 percent of all funeral services are religious, he will be conducting the service, giving the eulogy (if there is one), and comforting the bereaved as is his pastoral function. More than the funeral director, his specific function varies in each individual instance: precisely what his faith prescribes he do, what he is permitted to do, and what in fact he actually does.

If the one who died was active in the church and the

clergyman knew the family well, even as a close friend, his involvement is very great and exceedingly personal, and his support and comfort is direct and heartfelt. But if the family was not so active in the church or if they had only perfunctory contact with the minister, then his help and involvement is much more limited. The funeral becomes a part of his already crowded calendar of already scheduled activities, and his actions will be correct but understandably not too involved. Because he does not know the family or its friends or its general life values, his words or actions can just as easily offend as help, as he himself is very much aware. His portion of the activity is usually limited to performing the religious rites held in the church or funeral home chapel.

And should the family not be regular churchgoers at all but still want the funeral held under church sanction, the relationship with the minister can be fairly strained. He on one hand may feel his presence is superfluous, a perfunctory gesture that's demeaning to his calling. The family, on the other hand, may find his presence uncomfortable, and his support too often consisting of remonstrances for lax behavior in the past rather than meaningful comfort at this time of strain.

Often the important people who take over the day-to-day work until the funeral is over are relatives and close friends. They perform the chores and details involved in handling visitors from out of town, or the friends and colleagues who come at various times and at various stages of the ritual to attend the ceremonies, pay their respects, and give condolences. They are close enough to the one who died or the family to have personal compassion and concern; yet are not so grief-stricken as to be hindered in doing the many tasks that must be done.

The chores they perform are myriad. They may have to call

up other family members, particularly those out of town, also friends, an employer, or business colleagues and organizations, to tell them of the death and when and where visiting hours and the funeral will be held. They can be on hand at the house, in the funeral home, or at the church to greet people at the door, answer the phone, and keep a record of people who make condolence calls in person or by phone. They can keep the house clean, do the necessary shopping, do cooking, and put up coffee (or organize offerings of food others bring), feed the children and put them to bed on time, pick up out-of-town visitors and friends from airports and bus stations, see that the out-of-towners are housed and fed, and make sure the ordinary day-to-day business of the house is kept up (including the feeding of pets and the watering of the plants) while the rest of the family is in seclusion or involved with the funeral proceedings.

One chore they usually take over is the supervision of the children. The degree and nature of the participation of the children in the funeral vary. Many clergymen and lay persons feel strongly that children should not be excluded from observing, even from participating, in the rites. Others feel that children should be somewhat shielded, the degree of involvement limited both in time and contact. Still others go to great lengths to remove children from all such activities.

THE RELIGIOUS FUNERAL

The following is an overview of the religious funeral ritual as practiced by the three major religious faiths in the United States. By knowing what to anticipate, a person can prepare for possible moments of stress, can recognize the customary procedure, and see the deviations made in the norm.

While in general each religious faith has its own particular format, including variations within the faith itself, there is a pattern common to them all.

Protestantism, with its acknowledged pluralism, shows the greatest amount of variation among and within its many denominations, both in the format of the rite and the procedure preceding and following the service. Protestants in general, says one prominent clergyman, do not adhere to any special or unique custom other than the practice of having a funeral and a committal service.

The viewing of the body before the funeral service, to pay respects to the dead and offer condolences to the family, is customary but by no means a universal practice. This visitation period (also called "calling hours" or "lying in state") almost always is held in the funeral home, although in the past and on rare occasions now it still is held in the private home. The calling hours span from one to four days preceding the funeral, depending on local custom and the need for an extended period to accommodate all who would come to view the body. If there are friends of the family who live long distances from the funeral home or who have heavy social schedules, alternative days and hours are needed in order to allow everyone who wishes to make an appearance. Sometimes different groups are asked to come on different nights: one evening for lodge members to hold their special funeral ritual, another for business colleagues and professional friends, still another reserved just for family. The pattern of large numbers of people coming over many days appears typical more of the East, Midwest, and the South than of the Far West. There the practice is usually confined to the night before the funeral.

One or more members of the family are always present to receive the condolences of the visitors during the designated hours, and frequently all are present. Sometimes the chairs are set in a formal row pattern facing the casket in front, with the family seated either in the front rows or in an adjoining room or alcove. At other times the casket is in a niche on the side of the room or in an adjoining room to the one where the visitors congregate. Flowers may be banked around the casket or displayed all around the room. The atmosphere tends to be informal. In fact, one type of calling hours known as the memorial reception, popular in the Far West, is extremely informal, with chairs placed in a circular or even more haphazard fashion, food often on the sideboard, and friends and the family commingling in casual fashion, exchanging reminiscences about the one who died. The open casket is either in an adjoining room or on the far side of the reception room.

It's the custom, when people come to the funeral home, to sign the visitors' book, pay their respects at the casket, and then attend the immediate family to offer their condolences. Friends send flowers to the funeral home unless specifically forbidden to do so. Sometimes people are asked to make a memorial gift to a specified or general charity in lieu of flowers, but flowers frequently are sent anyway.

Visitors remain to talk with the family for as long as they care to, then they commingle with others in the room. The occasion is usually social, not religious, although various Pentecostal groups use the calling hours as occasions for vocal and active lamentation, while the Evangelical denominations frequently read Scripture, say prayers, or sing hymns.

It is customary for some member of the family to remain throughout the designated hours, although the principal mourner may retire after a certain period of attendance.

The Protestant funeral service, which follows the visitation,

is traditionally held in the church building, although on occasion the service is held in the funeral home chapel, sometimes even in the home.

The casket is brought to the front of the church, and may
or may not be open during the service, depending on the
wishes of the immediate family and the clergyman. The
elements of the service vary. Often the ritual is determined
by the book of worship of that particular denomination. It
may consist, in part or wholly, of a reading of Scripture, offerings of prayer, a sermon or meditation, and perhaps a
eulogy. Selections of verse or biblical quotations, appropriate
organ music, sometimes hymns sung by the congregation are
also included. A newer variation is the contemporary funeral
worship service at which nonconventional music or instruments are used and more modern selections are read instead
of or in addition to traditional scriptural ones.

When the service is over, if the casket is open it is customary for the congregants who so wish to file by the casket
to pay their final respects.

There are three major variations to this formal funeral
service, all of recent origin. One is the religious memorial
service, identical to the funeral ceremony, except that by
design the casket is not present. (The committal of the body
either took place in a private ceremony before the memorial
service or will take place after the service is concluded, with
only the immediate family in attendance.)

The second, one step removed, is the nonreligious or humanist service for persons baptized as Protestants but with
no current church affiliation. By predeath request or at the
request of the next of kin after the death a minister presides
over the ceremony but the content of the service is without
religious references. (One such service manual has been developed by Rev. Paul Irion.) The casket may or may not be
present; if present, it may or may not be open.

The third alternative is the memorial service, held after the body has already been cremated or buried. Regarded less as a Protestant service than a nonsectarian one, this will be described later in the chapter.

After the church service the casket is taken to the hearse and a procession of mourners drives out to the cemetery where a brief committal service, a continuation and final portion of the church funeral service, is held at graveside. While for various reasons the service sometimes is not held at graveside but concluded at the church, many denominations regard the committal service as a final rite signifying the breaking of all ties with the dead, and as such requiring the enactment at the grave.

After the committal ceremony the family returns home. What happens at this point is largely unstructured. Some communities have an established custom of the closest friends bringing food and gathering to eat with the family. Other communities, in the Midwest particularly, have established a church custom of having all church members participate in potluck dinner with the family as a gesture of communal concern. In still other places there is no visitation after the funeral at all; all sympathy calls take place during the visitation before the funeral. After the funeral, the family withdraws for a while—and chooses its own time to come back into society.

The pattern of what occurs in the months that follow is also largely unstructured. Often church members continue to visit and offer consolation, and the clergy tends to give more regular counseling and attention to the bereaved.

THE ROMAN CATHOLIC FUNERAL

Among Roman Catholics the form and structure of the funeral rites are more ritualized and uniform throughout the

country, although there are cultural and community variations.

The first part of the ritual starts as soon as possible after
death with the body laid out after embalming. This is the
wake, the "vigil or period of waiting for the funeral itself."
At one time the wake was held in the family home and in
some places still is, although it's much more usual today for
the wake to be held in the funeral home itself. It usually
lasts one or two days. It is the time when friends, colleagues,
lodge brothers, union and business associates gather to pay
their last respects to the dead and give condolences to the
family. Many send flowers to the wake; others leave cards
announcing a Mass being said for the dead, or indicating a
donation to a charity.

The casket may be open or closed, the floral arrangements
lavish or restrained, the atmosphere formal or very informal.
At some designated hour during the evening, a wake service
is held by the priest, which includes readings of the Scripture
and prayers. A rosary devotional, once very common at
wakes, may still be observed in some places.

At the Catholic wake, the procedure for friends is to sign
the visitors' book, go directly to the family first to give them
words of sympathy, then move to the casket to kneel or
offer a brief prayer.

In the past wakes were quite elaborate affairs; and when
held in the home were accompanied by food and drink. Today, according to one authority, the trend is toward simplicity,
although some still incline to elaborate ritual, particularly in
those cultural groups where these rituals remain meaningful
to an older generation.

The funeral itself is a prayer service incorporated into the
celebration of Mass. Most friends gather at the church, but
the casket is brought from the funeral home in a procession
to the church by members of the immediate family and the

closest friends; there it's met at the door by the priest and then brought down the aisle. The service itself includes opening prayers, Bible readings, a homily (not a eulogy) by the priest, the eucharist prayer, and communion. The Mass closes with the rite of commendation. Music accompanies the service.

After the Mass a formal funeral procession accompanies the hearse to the cemetery where a brief public committal rite is held. As a rule, the family does not remain at the cemetery for the burial itself, although in some areas it is becoming common for the family to remain until the body is lowered into the grave.

After the committal ceremony the family goes home, sometimes accompanied by a small group of friends. Condolence calls at the home after the burial are not customary, although this varies with the locality. The clergy, however, make formalized counseling available to the family in the months that follow. A month after the death a Month's Mass is celebrated. Thereafter anniversary Masses are often arranged by the family on each successive anniversary of death.

THE JEWISH FUNERAL

The most fundamentalist of the Jewish denominations, the Orthodox, adheres to an extremely ritualized format for the funeral, the burial, and the mourning period. The Conservative and Reform denominations, each successively more liberal than the Orthodox, participate in those forms which are established customary Jewish practices. However, the degree of conformity depends on the denominational position and the inclination and formalized religious commitment of the family.

Immediately after death there are certain ritualistic activities the Orthodox Jews engage in concerning the cleansing and preparation of the body and other mortuary customs that funeral directors are familiar with.

Ordinarily there is no visiting at the home of the immediate family before the funeral. Sometimes the body is laid out in the funeral home the night before the funeral for friends and acquaintances to come to pay their respects to the family, but the traditional time for condolence calls is after the funeral. Also, there usually is no time before the funeral. By tradition the body is buried very quickly, the time depending primarily on how soon the family can be gathered together. It is not unusual for burial to be completed within twenty-four to forty-eight hours; seldom is it held more than three or four days after death.

The rabbi conducts the religious service, which customarily is held in the chapel of the funeral home, *not* the synagogue or temple, although there is a trend, particularly among Reform Jews, to hold it in the place of worship.

Flowers are not customary condolence offerings at Jewish funerals, although flowers sent by non-Jewish friends of the family as an expression of sympathy are of course accepted in the spirit in which they are given. Contributions to charity or sympathy cards or letters are acceptable, although attendance at the funeral or at the home after the funeral is the customary gesture of sympathy.

Because the Jewish funeral is primarily a rite of separation, the presence of the casket, open or closed, is required. The service consists of prayers, often the reading of the Twenty-third Psalm, a symbolic rending of the clothes of the mourners, and a eulogy of the dead. At the conclusion of the service an automobile entourage proceeds from the chapel to the cemetery, where a commital ceremony at graveside is conducted. Attendance in the processional and at the grave are expected of well-wishers as expressions of community support for the bereaved and respect for the dead.

A formalized period of mourning held at the home of the family begins as soon as the burial is concluded. It is called the Shiva (seven) because traditionalists require that the bereaved family sit in mourning for seven days while friends and neighbors call continuously to offer condolences, bring food, eat together, join in ritualized prayers, and talk with the bereaved about the dead. The less traditional denominations permit a three-day mourning period to suffice, and sometimes even less. Children are often encouraged to participate, even being asked to help with the greeting duties; this, of course, depends on the age of the child, closeness to the one who died, and family wishes.

Orthodox Jews then have a traditional thirty-day mourning of restricted activity after the Shiva, but if the one who died is a parent, the mourning continues for an entire year. Jews of other denominations adhere less rigidly to these observances. Thereafter the anniversary of the death is marked by special prayers. A separate dedication of the gravestone or plaque (the "unveiling") takes place within the first year. Friends of the family are invited to attend just as they were to the original funeral service.

THE MEMORIAL SERVICE

Other forms and rituals departing from these familiar religious ones have recently been developed by people and organizations disenchanted with the content of the older forms who feel the need for less stereotyped, more individualized commemoration rituals when death takes place. The memorial service is one that the more liberal branches of Protestantism, some of the more liberal Jewish congregations, and a great many who profess no formal religious commitment follow. It takes place after the immediate cremation or burial of the body.

There is no "format" for the memorial service. It can be

held from a few days to a few weeks after the death occurred. It is held at the church or in the funeral home, in the home or any other place the family or friends feel is appropriate. Music is usually played. Sometimes a clergyman gives a eulogy; at other times, others arise and speak in eulogy-type fashion about their friend. Friends speak from a lectern or from the audience, where the chairs are arranged in rows, or in a circle, or in more informal groupings. The sentiments expressed either are on the good works of the one who died or consist of consoling the family who remains. Sometimes vocal prayers are offered; sometimes silent meditation takes place. The request for memorial gifts or charitable contributions rather than flowers as preferred channels by which friends can offer condolences is common.

After the funeral or memorial service, there still remain the courtesy gestures that conclude all social rites: the family's acknowledgment of the flowers, gifts, memorial donations, or special prayers given by friends and colleagues. These are answered by handwritten note or by cards furnished by the funeral director; and if no one else can do this, the funeral director himself does so as the final part of his service.

19

Immediate Postdeath Arrangements

The funeral is over. And while the ritualized mourning period may not be, you still must take care of the unresolved details that remain.

DISPOSING OF PERSONAL PROPERTY

If you can, now is a good time to give away clothing and personal belongings of your spouse or parent. There's always more than seems possible for one person to have accumulated: clothes, toiletries, costume jewelry, bags and shoes, need-to-be-repaired tape recorders, typewriters, cameras, sewing machines, workshop equipment, garden supplies, and so forth.

Ask friends and relatives if they can put these belongings to good use. If not give them to charity. Sometimes the nursing home or hospital has a volunteer thrift shop where these possessions of little extrinsic value can be sold. Don't simply throw them into the rubbish bin just to get them out of sight.

Personal papers and printed accumulations must also be culled. You've already removed the important ones: insurance policies, bills to be paid, checks and tax returns, documents of all kinds. The residue consists of books, pamphlets, magazines, clippings for future reference, undecipherable memoranda, reference notes of all kinds, recipes and household accounts, old correspondence and archives, college papers and notes, high school yearbooks and old love letters.

Throw out what you can; store the rest in a closet or attic for future culling. There's no need for immediate and drastic house cleaning right now. Psychologists differ as to the best time to start the casting-off process.

What they *don't* differ about is the inadvisability of keeping these visual reminders of the dead always around. The "mummification" of memories through the constant presence and active preservation of the artifacts of the dead hinders rather than helps the necessary readjustment to life ahead.

The larger, more costly possessions that remain—the house, furniture, car—pose a different problem. These have appreciable monetary value. They're part of the estate and can be disposed of at your discretion only if owned in such a way that they pass into your possession without becoming involved in any proceedings. This would be, for example, a house held in joint tenancy with right of survivorship. This will be discussed in the next chapter.

But even if these possessions are yours to sell, delay your decision if at all possible, unless an economic need requires you sell them. Too often persons divest themselves of these large belongings quickly in order "to forget." Only later on do they realize, to their regret, that these possessions represented important rocks of security that they sorely miss—as do their children.

FINANCES

Though the problems of adjustment are intricately involved with finances, it's the finances and not the adjustment that must concern you at the moment. There's no bereavement that isn't easier to bear if there is no financial pressure in day-to-day living. How you go about easing the pressure that already exists varies with your age, the number of your dependents, your present money resources, and your immediate prospects for a steady income.

There are long-range projections you must eventually make. Right now, however, you're still focusing on the short run: how to get immediate pecuniary help for yourself and your dependents for perhaps the next year or until the estate is unencumbered and available to you.

A good lawyer can be of inestimable value to you in this immediate period after the death. He or she can relieve you of a great deal of complicating detail at a time when you can use the help. For example, the attorney certainly can assist in opening your closed joint bank account so you can get immediate cash until more money becomes available; can look for the will; can gather together the important documents you need to make claim for social security annuities, VA lump-sum benefits, and any insurance claims; and can check out all the company benefits coming to you: insurance, salary continuance programs, profit-sharing and pension plan benefits, and so on.

If you have a personal friend who is a lawyer, turn to him or her for help. If you don't know one personally and you are worried about what the legal fees will be, go see an attorney and ask. He or she can give you an estimate on how much time may be involved and generally what the upper limit of the fee will be. Even an attorney who feels you can help yourself still will give you hints on going about the job that may be helpful.

But if there's no one to help you at this time, then take care of matters on your own. You still might need legal expertise at crucial times, so have a friend give you the name of someone you can call in an emergency.

If you worry about probate proceedings keeping you in financial straits for what you understand will be a full year, bear in mind that there are certain assets available to you now that fall outside the probate process. Some of these are available for immediate cash, others will be forthcoming as cash or income as soon as you apply for them. The sooner you take care of collecting this immediate cash and income, the quicker you can turn your attention to getting the bulk of the estate released.

FUNDS IMMEDIATELY AVAILABLE

Joint Bank Accounts. Some states (and within permitting states, some banks) allow you to continue to draw money from a joint checking account even if one of the parties has died. Others seal the checking account just as they do a joint savings account. However, according to lawyers who deal with these matters, the spectre of being cut off from all cash resources after a death is largely unfounded—unless you've always lived on such a thin edge of penury that getting hold of cash has always been a problem.

If you have a checking account and there's not so much in it that would cause the tax agents to believe it's being used as a tax-evasion cash outlet, a conference with the bank manager will surely allow a reasonable withdrawal. If not, the help of an attorney will get some funds released within twenty-four hours. An attorney, in fact, can also unblock a savings account from which you can draw a reasonable amount as necessary, just as long as what remains appears to be enough to pay whatever taxes are required. Your real problem is not getting the money *out* of the accounts, but getting money in!

U.S. Savings Bonds. Savings bonds in your possession that name you as beneficiary can be cashed at a bank upon proof of the purchaser's death (a certified copy of the death certificate). But bank tellers are not as knowledgeable about this process as they might be. Go to a large Federal Reserve bank for the quickest processing. Otherwise you may be shunted from one teller to another, to the assistant manager to the operations manager to the vice president. In the end, the bank itself will have to send the application to the Federal Reserve bank, which will further delay payment.

Bank or Credit Union Loan. It may be that just at the moment the death took place, a large amount of cash was needed (e.g., your child's college tuition was due that week). Apply immediately for a loan at the bank, savings and loan association, or credit union. Ordinarily there is a time lag; but if your spouse had good credit, if the extenuating circumstances are explained, and it's apparent that there's insurance and other money coming in eventually, you should have it approved forthwith. Ask your attorney to help expedite it if you have any trouble. Otherwise go directly to the people to whom the money is due, and see if you can get a time extension until the loan is approved.

ANNUITY PAYMENTS

Social Security. If you are eligible for social security annuity payments, as soon as your claim is validated and processed your benefits will start to come to you in regular monthly payments. Processing may take a few months though, so the sooner you make your claim the quicker the checks start coming.

Social security payments often are associated only with retirement, but there is a vast program of monthly payments that is available to survivors as well. Briefly, as applied to your present circumstances, you are eligible for an annuity if:

1. you are an unmarried surviving child under the age of eighteen (or age twenty-two if a full-time student);

2. you are an unmarried surviving child over eighteen who was severely disabled before the age of twenty-two and are still disabled;

3. you are a widow or dependent widower sixty years old or older;

4. you are a widowed mother, a widower father, or a surviving divorced mother taking care of a child under eighteen (or a disabled child) who is getting a benefit based on the earnings of the one who died;

5. you are a widow or dependent widower fifty years old or older who is now disabled;

6. you are a dependent parent sixty-two years old or older;

7. you are a surviving divorced wife sixty years old or older, or a disabled surviving divorced wife fifty years old or older, if the marriage lasted twenty years or more.

There are even certain circumstances in which you are entitled to social security benefits based on the earnings of a *grandparent* who died. Obviously all these possibilities bear looking into.

Widowed fathers caring for minor or disabled children now are entitled to social security benefits on the records of their deceased wives, according to a March 1975 decision of the Supreme Court. What was previously a sex-discrimination feature of the social security law (against men) has now been removed.

However, there are still restrictions in the law that limit or prevent benefits from being paid. If two or more children are already receiving benefits from one social security record, the total family benefits may not increase if the father becomes eligible. Also a father's benefits, like a mother's, are affected by his earnings. If the surviving spouse earns over a minimum of $2,520 in a year, he or she loses one dollar in benefits for every two dollars over that amount. And the benefits generally end if he or she marries.

If you haven't yet made a claim for the benefits due you, call your local social security office. The officers there will explain precisely what documentation is needed to substantiate the claim, whether to mail the papers in or bring them in, the exact amount of benefits to which you're entitled, and when to expect the first check.

Government Programs "In Lieu Of . . ." If your spouse was excluded from coverage under social security but was covered under other government programs, call the local office of the agency or department in which he or she worked to find out what benefits you are entitled to. You may already have heard from them. Usually when someone dies the personnel office automatically notifies the office in charge of survivors' benefits to begin the paperwork. But the wheels of bureaucracy grind slowly, and a direct inquiry may get the claim moving a little faster.

Company Pension or Profit-Sharing Plans. By now you should have been contacted by the company if your spouse was part of either of these programs. In either, there may be a survivor's death benefit or group insurance provision as an integral part of the setup. If you have heard nothing, call them immediately for further information. If you have no name or specific office to call, contact the company personnel office.

Union Pension and Welfare Funds. Many of the large AFL-CIO unions have health, welfare, and pension programs that provide generous benefits to the survivors of members who died. Some are industry-wide programs independent of any particular company. Check through your spouse's papers for the specific name of the person or office you can call for cash or an annuity. (Perhaps one of his work colleagues can tell you the name of the person in charge.) Otherwise call union headquarters and explain to whomever answers what you are calling for. Eventually you'll be routed to the right person who will send you whatever papers are necessary.

Sometimes the plan is one jointly funded and administered by the union and company. In this case your call to the company will direct you to the office where the program is administered.

In any case, whether the program is joint or separate, check, recheck, and double-check until the forms are filled out and processed, and the checks actually start coming to you.

CLAIMING INSURANCE BENEFITS

Gather together all the life insurance policies and certificates you can find. Don't forget to include any one-time special insurance that may have been taken out, particularly a policy connected with the death, such as a travelers' insurance policy taken out at the airport (which was probably received in the mail). If the death was accidental, the double-indemnity clauses in this and other policies are of vital importance.

USING A BROKER OR DOING IT YOURSELF

Before you start writing away for claims on your own, you may want to ask your insurance broker to take charge of the entire matter. It isn't that the problem is particularly complicated—it's just that the paperwork is time-consuming, the personal contact sometimes may be exasperating, and perhaps you're not as ready to cope as you might be.

An insurance broker can check through all the insurance policies that you have, and perhaps even discover some applicable group term insurance you knew nothing about. Also, there may be insurance benefits accruing as part of the company's profit-sharing plan or pension plan, or union pension plan, which a broker can locate even better than an attorney. There may be provisions in the medical insurance policies your spouse had that can take care of some of the outstanding medical debts you've been worrying about. Moreover, a broker's help as early as possible will get the life insurance claims filed quickly so that the claims can be readily processed.

However, if you feel you want to handle the details yourself, then do the following:

1. Check each policy to see if you are the beneficiary. If someone other than you is named, then you cannot claim the money. However, if the beneficiary appears to be someone who was inadvertently retained as an oversight (an ex-spouse, perhaps), talk with your attorney. Maybe the named beneficiary is amenable to negotiation on the proceeds.

2. Of the policies that name you beneficiary, check the premium receipts to see if they were in force when death occurred. However, don't throw any away just because it looks as if the premiums haven't been paid and the policies

lapsed. Dividends may have accumulated to pay the premiums automatically, or the policy may still provide some, if not all, benefits. Make claim to the company anyway.

3. Check each policy to see if it indicates specifically how the money is to be paid out at death. If it does, that's how you will receive the money. Unless otherwise indicated by a specific policy option, you have a choice of how you want the money given to you.

INSURANCE OPTIONS

Generally you have six alternatives, as the insurance agents will point out to you later when you file a claim. You can:

1. receive the face value of the policy in one lump-sum payment;

2. leave the money on deposit with the insurance company and collect interest at regular, periodic intervals, the principal remaining intact for later withdrawal at request;

3. receive the money in specific monthly installments until the principal and interest run out;

4. receive the money in installments for a specified length of time, at the end of which the principal and the interest will have been distributed.

5. choose a life annuity whose increments are based on the mortality table figures (which may or may not end up in your favor, depending on how long you live); or

6. choose an annuity for a specified number of years, with a second beneficiary receiving the remainder of the money if you should die before you receive the final payment.

Usually if you choose any option other than the first and the last two, you can change your mind and withdraw all or part of whatever is left at any time. Also, the purchaser of the policy may have included a clause in the policy giving you a limited right to get a cash advance against the principal in case you need a large amount of money at any time. This includes the annuity options, of course.

The overwhelming number of beneficiaries (85.6 percent) choose to receive the lump-sum face value immediately. Many then redeposit it in a bank or look to invest it in some income-producing stock or property. But despite the popularity of this option, there are a number of drawbacks at this particular time.

The first is that widows and widowers both are prime targets for swindles by characters who read obituary columns, attend public funerals, and determine who the people are who have received large sums of insurance cash.

The common confidence games have been repeatedly exposed on television or in popular magazines, but each year thousands more become victims to these fraudulent schemes. The "pigeon drop," the "diamond-switch swindle," and the bank-examiner fraud are three among many. In each, a pair of seeming strangers persuade the victim to draw out cash from a savings account to purchase something of greater value. Then the two abscond with the money and the windfall the victim expects never materializes.

But of much greater danger to you is not the deliberate swindle but risky and unwise investment suggested by friends, friends of friends, colleagues, or investment counselors. Often the promised high rate of return on the principal doesn't materialize, and sometimes the principal is lost as well. One shocking figure shows that 80 percent of all life insurance paid out in cash is gone within one year of the death. Another estimate claims only 60 percent is dissipated within *two* years, and even that is bad enough. To run such a risk when your discernment faculties still are not at their sharpest hardly seems wise.

On the other hand, the need for cash on hand may be pressing—and insurance companies are usually very prompt in processing claims. You may find you will *need* the cash just to meet day-to-day expenses for months on end.

However if you don't, you might consider leaving the proceeds with the insurance company and taking the interest payments until you get a better picture of your entire financial future.

Write to the various life insurance companies and request their claims forms. Meanwhile ask the funeral director to get for you certified copies of the death certificate from the county clerk. You'll need one copy for every claim. (You'll need copies for other purposes also. For every transaction from now on that requires proof of death, you'll need a certified copy. Try to estimate how many you'll need now; they may cost a few dollars each. Otherwise you must ask for additional copies later.)

You've already checked out the small face-value policies from certain insurance companies and from fraternal clubs and lodges in connection with funeral and burial expenses. Now you must look into the possibility of bigger term policies that may exist.

GROUP TERM LIFE INSURANCE

Job-Related. If you can't find the name of the person to call regarding any on-the-job group insurance, and no one has called you from your spouse's company or from the insurance company, call the company personnel office, explain to them who you are, and ask to talk to someone about the group insurance and coverage. They will either give you the name of someone to contact, will get the information for you and send you the forms, or will set up an appointment for you to speak to the people who will get the claim started for you.

Professional Groups. Even if you can't find an actual policy, premium receipt, or explanatory brochure pointing to the existence of such a policy, don't presume there isn't any. Professional and affinity organizations (American Association of University Women, the Institute of Electrical and Electronics Engineers, and the Writers Guild of America, to name just a few at random) frequently offer such a group policy as a fringe benefit of membership. Inquire of all the organizations your spouse belonged to that appear even likely; this is the only way you'll find out if such insurance exists. You may even get a lead to a benefit that *they* didn't know you were entitled to!

These immediate funds come to you even though technically they may be part of the estate (with the exception of social security, of course). This is irrespective of whether or not the deceased left anything else to you as beneficiary or whether there was a will or not. Income annuities, life insurance, and pension plan residuals come to you outside the inheritance process.

But your inheritance is a very important part of your family's financial future. The following chapters delineate how you're to get that.

20

Settling the Small Estate

In most cases your spouse has left what can be termed an estate. Unless he or she has lived a hand-to-mouth existence (and with dependents, that's not too likely), there is some property, often both real and personal. Usually there is more than you imagine. In some cases there will be much more.

Whether the estate is large or small, you should locate the will as quickly as possible, for in most states the will must be filed with the probate clerk within a very short time (one to three weeks). If one can't be found, the clerk must be notified that there is no will.

The will is essential. You may think not if you're convinced the total estate is very small or that in any case you—as spouse—would inherit it all, will or no. Neither presumption may be true. There's almost no circumstance where it's not better to *have* a will than *not* to have one; so look for it wherever you think it may be located.

Ordinarily a will is kept by the attorney who drew it up, with a copy in the safe deposit box. You should know who this attorney is (although it's amazing how many spouses who claim they were close to their partners in every way have no idea who the family attorney is).

Sometimes the original will is in the safe deposit box in the bank or in a metal safety box in the desk at home. Or it may be in a bureau drawer, in a file cabinet drawer (or under the mattress, or behind the file cabinet).

Search for the will in all these places and every other one you can think of. If you can't find it, write or telephone the lawyer your spouse may have used in the city where you once lived, who may have drawn up the papers years ago. Check with his or her business associates to see if anyone remembers the will, or perhaps witnessed its signing. Don't stop searching until you're absolutely certain there is none.

If there is no will, then the transfer of property may become complicated by the probate process—particularly if the property is intricate, if your relationship with the one who died is not a simple one, or if your need for funds is pressing.

The probate court, known by other names in various states, supervises the transfer or distribution of the assets of the deceased's estate to whomever it should go, as laid down by the will or determined by state statute if there is no will.

Possibly because the procedures in the court appear routine, unhurried, and impersonal, and because the procedures outside the court fall into the fiscal and legal area preempted by experts, lay people often see the probate process as a needlessly expensive and time-consuming intrusion on the business of ordinary people. One critic calls it "the only situation today where we are forced to go to court even though there is no controversy."

Attorneys who work in this area, however, feel that the malevolence of probate, like the fear of the sealed bank account, has been highly overstated. They claim the work is fraught with legal pitfalls though it may appear routine, and costly litigation can tie up the estate for years. Other lawyers state that the outcry is unjustified simply because a significant part of all small- and medium-sized estates often pass directly to the heirs without being involved in probate at all.

Estates of $20,000 or less usually don't even reach the lower boundary of state taxation. In many states the tax exemption is higher; and the federal government's estate tax interest doesn't start until $60,000, for the estate of a single person, or $120,000, if the person who died was married and the spouse claims the marital deduction. Estates of gross amounts even higher than this often avoid the probate process with various exemptions, deductions, and tax-avoidance devices.

At any rate, even though the Uniform Probate Code proposed in 1969 to reduce delays and cost is in effect in only eleven states, many states have simplified and streamlined their probate requirements and procedures within the last ten years to correct the most flagrant cases of injustice. Some actual probate processes have been simplified in some cases. But in most states the new procedures usually pertain to "small" estates, exempting them from probate proceedings entirely.

The key word is "usually." Whether or not it becomes necessary to go into probate court to settle what is in essence a fairly small, simple estate, and one where there may be no will, depends on the form in which the property is held, on the size of the estate, and the laws of that particular state.

If there is no will, you may fall in that category of persons who inherit a small- or medium-sized estate that will pass directly to you as an heir without being subject to probate at all.

If the estate is really small there is no question of your spouse's assets passing directly to you. If, for example, your husband had retired and the two of you were living on his pension and social security income, after his death survivor's annuities will now come to you. Your minimal personal property is of no interest to the state. What you have belongs to you and need not be submitted to probate.

Some states provide even further protection when the estate is very small. Under a shield called "an award in lieu of homestead" (or "the family allowance" or simply "the exemption"), a protected area of your estate is marked off-limits from creditors, even when their claims are legitimate. Its purpose was, and is, to protect the impoverished family by providing a minimum estate that no one could deprive them of, in order that they not be left completely destitute. Although in some states the amount qualifying for such protected status has been raised by legislative statute to as high as $10,000, it is clearly designed for the minimal estate.

At the outset, remember that some assets of the estate pass to you directly: property held in joint tenancy, annuities, U.S. savings bonds, and insurance. Even though all are assets of the gross estate (with the exception of some pension-fund annuities), they should pose no problem as far as settling the estate is concerned.

If the property is mostly of this kind, the transfer can be done with minimum difficulty and with minimal interference. All life insurance payable to you as survivor can be claimed. If there are U.S. bonds payable to you as survivor you can go to the bank to fill out the forms to transfer the bonds to your name. The house is already yours. To settle up the rest you go to the bank and open up a new savings account in your own name and get permission from the bank officer to transfer the money from the joint accounts into yours. If there are outstanding bills, you pay them, including current household debts, the last hospital bill, and the funeral expenses. This probably is all that is necessary. (You might want to consult a lawyer to make sure you've touched all legal bases. Perhaps there is a state inheritance tax form that must be filed even though there is no money due.)

If a check of your spouse's property turns up more personal property than you thought there was, then you must find out if your state has a simplified process for transferring such property without going through an extended probate procedure.

When the estate is small (and "small" is interpreted by legislative statute as anywhere from $500 to $10,000) and consisting mainly of personal property below that legislative ceiling, states permit the transfer of property by the small estates affidavit. Whoever is legally entitled to the property simply signs a small estates affidavit stating that the estate assets are under the ceiling provided by law. This affidavit is then delivered to whomever is holding the property; this person, in turn, signs over the property to the intended owner. A small estates affidavit can be filed even if there is no will, providing only personal property is involved.

If there is real property, a will may be necessary in order to prove you are entitled to the property. If there is a will and there is real property, some states permit a spouse to file a petition with the court through an attorney stating that the *net* value of the estate, after liens and encumbrances are deducted, is less than the legislative limit. If the court is satisfied that this is the case, it will order the transfer of these assets directly to the spouse and children.

But if a will is required and there is no will in your case, then the matter will have to be filed in probate court for disposition. Now the matter of relationship becomes crucial. For intestacy estates the laws of the states only recognize inheritance by marriage or by blood relationship—and such laws are inflexible and not always fair. You may find, for example, that even if you are a spouse you will not necessarily inherit the entire estate. You may have to share with your children, even if grown or estranged, or with your spouse's parents. If you are not a close relation (perhaps a cousin or a niece), even though you may have taken care of the person who died and most certainly would have been named an heir in any executed will, you may still be deprived of any property from the estate if there are persons closer in relationship who stand higher on the chart of intestate succession than you. And should you not have been related by marriage or a blood relationship at all, the lack of a will deprives you entirely of claim to any probated assets.

If the estate falls under the jurisdiction of the probate court, either because there is no will or because the property left does not bypass the probate proceedings, then you are subject to the legal strictures of the state in which you live. Consult an attorney and find out what you must do as required by law. Whether the probate process is necessary to protect the heirs—particularly minor children—creditors, and the state from unscrupulous persons, as those who support it contend, or whether it's a ripoff of the nonlegal world by the legal profession, as its outspoken critics maintain, is beside the point at the moment.

You have just been through a death in the family, and now you must get someone else's affairs straightened out, to say nothing of your own. The timing of this probate involvement is not the best in the world, but, as mentioned in connection with funeral reform, the time for probate reform, if indeed you feel it is needed, is not now. At the moment, your business is to do what has to be done. Have your lawyer help you get it completed as quickly and as painlessly as possible.

21

The Large Estate and Executor Duties

The larger the estate, the more essential the will, and presumably any person with an estate large enough to require the payment of federal taxes would have had the foresight to draw up a will and keep it updated. Unfortunately, this is not always the case. However, if your spouse or parent left no will there is little you can do about it at this point. The estate assets will be redistributed in any event, just as in the case of the smaller estate: according to the wishes of the one who died if there is a will or according to the dictates of the state statute if he or she died without a will. It may be that you will be intricately involved in that distribution as executor or administrator of the estate.

The executor or executrix named in the will is the one responsible for managing the after-death affairs of the deceased and eventually distributing his or her property according to the instructions given in the will. If there is no will, the court appoints an administrator or administratrix to perform approximately the same functions.

When the will was drawn up originally, the person who did so was of course under no obligation to name the closest next of kin as executor; nor is a probate court always required to give preference to the closest next of kin when appointing an administrator for an intestacy estate, although it frequently does. (In fact, the strong chance that the probate court will appoint the next of kin who may lack legal skills or business acumen needed to administer the estate is the spectre financial advisors point to when extolling the need for drawing up a will in the first place.)

If indeed you now find you are the primary beneficiary but *not* the estate executor or administrator, make sure the attorney for the estate explains to you precisely what the executor will do, what is likely to happen as far as the estate assets are concerned, and how long all the actions involved will take. Above all, make sure both the attorney and the executor explain in detail all financial matters that concern you (even though they may hint broadly that it's all too complicated and you'd probably not be interested in any event). You may require a family allowance (which will be explained shortly) to provide funds to live on until the estate is settled. The responsibility of the children may also require that the family allowance be supplemented later on if extraordinary demands arise. Find out if and under what circumstances this may be forthcoming.

The duties of the executor or administrator are no different for a member of the family than for an outsider. But if you are related to the one who died, then you have an additional burden if you *are* the executor. Your duties will have to be carried out while you are still in bereavement. The funeral was just the prelude to a new phase: a long, sometimes very involved, time-consuming and painstaking process of property settlement.

Although you may be named in the will as the executor,

you have the prerogative of refusing the job if you feel you simply cannot do what is required. If you do and the will provides no alternates, understand that the probate court will appoint an administrator to act in your stead; and the costs against the estate (including a surety bond, which may have been waived with you as executor) will be as though there were no will.

One factor determining whether you believe you can do the job will be how the death has affected you. If the death was an unexpected one, you may find the shock lingering for quite a while, rendering you incapable of proceeding quickly on the estate settlement. If an attorney or a bank is named coexecutor with you, they may have to carry on without you (but with your concurrence, of course) until you get over the roughest period, for many of the duties must be performed within a specified time limit.

But if the death was expected and a protracted period of anticipatory grief preceded the death, you may welcome the work involved by the time the funeral is over, eager to assume your duties as quickly as possible.

If you should decide to accept the role of executor or administrator, realize that you will be held personally responsible for the proper discharge of your duties as the decedent's personal representative. For this reason, if you are not yourself an attorney—and even if you are—you must work closely with capable experts who can help clear the way through the maze of state and federal government regulations, legal requirements, financial accounting procedures and filing deadlines, and special exceptions applicable to your specific estate situation.

You will need an attorney in settling the large estate. While the executor alone bears the responsibility, there are specified attorney-initiated actions required at various intervals during the probate proceedings, and mandatory in-court appearances that only a lawyer can make. (The exceptions to date are the states of Wisconsin and Minnesota, where noncontroversial probate proceedings can be handled entirely by lay persons). Some of these legal actions take place simultaneous with other work the executor performs; some must be done at set times before the following step can be taken. At all times the work of the lawyer and the executor must dovetail.

The choice of the attorney is yours to make, if you are the executor. (Even though an attorney is named in the will as coexecutor, it is possible, though not particularly likely, that you may feel the lawyer's legal acumen is sufficient to share the executor duties but not to bear the responsibility for the legal work. Who the attorney for the estate will be must then be resolved between the two of you.)

Frequently you will choose the attorney who handled the affairs of your spouse, parent, or friend in the past, perhaps even the one who drew up the will. This lawyer most likely is the one most familiar with the estate and its special and particular problems.

Since the attorney's commission for probating the will is either set by statute as a percentage of the value of the estate or is a fee determined as "reasonable" by the executor and the court, it ordinarily costs no more to have a good attorney than a poor one. You should get the best attorney you can.

Just how easy or difficult being an executor of a large estate will be depends not only on how complicated the estate is, but also on how well you and the lawyer work together. Initially you may be overwhelmed by what appears to be a forbidding and convoluted business. The attorney may have to spend much time, care, and patience explaining what must be done and often may be tempted to suggest that law clerks take some of the work off your hands.

However, you'll be better served in the long run by doing

what has to be done under the lawyer's supervision rather than having someone else do it for you. Even though at the beginning it may cost you—and the estate—more money (since an attorney's time is worth considerably more than the office help), the experience you get in handling these financial and business transactions may be invaluable in your life ahead as a single, independent, household head.

THE PROBATE PROCESS

The following is a general projection of what you as a lay executor can anticipate during the probate process.

The attorney starts the proceedings by petitioning the probate court in the state where the decedent lived to have the will admitted to probate. But your job as executor begins even before then.

It's possible that you'll hear for the first time that you've been named executor when the will is read; but this is unlikely. It is customary for the will-maker to get your permission first before naming you in the will.

Knowing that you were the named executor, you already were prepared for your first job as executor, that of helping with the funeral and burial arrangements. These were taken care of by the family—which included you if you are one of the family. If not, as executor, you probably were standing by to help as requested by the family during that harried time.

As executor it's your responsibility to notify all the beneficiaries of the will of what is due them. If the beneficiaries are located within a reasonable distance of each other or have come for the funeral, it's customary, although not required, to gather them together after the funeral and read the terms of the will aloud. In this way everyone is made familiar with the bequests left to everyone else.

If the will is going to be challenged, it probably will take place when the attorney submits the will to probate or shortly afterward. If this happens, the ensuing litigation becomes a lawyers' battle outside of your province. But in the vast majority of the cases, wills are not challenged.

At the time the will is submitted to probate, the attorney also petitions the court to appoint you executor. The judge then sets a court date for the hearing on your appointment. This may not take place for another three or four weeks, but since the hearing is usually *pro forma*, you can begin work on the assumption that the appointment will be made.

Your attorney should advise you at this point or later in the proceedings whether or not to waive the right to compensation as an executor. If you are also the principal or sole beneficiary, it may seem as though it makes no difference, but as a matter of fact it does, depending on rather intricate tax questions. Ask for advice if the attorney does not mention it.

While you are waiting for the court hearing, you may want to proceed to put in claims on the insurance policies naming you as beneficiary. Your attorney can help or you can do it on your own. Insurance companies usually are very prompt in processing claims, so this may ease some of the immediate financial pressures.

Then start your most important job as executor: preparing an inventory of all the assets of the estate.

Start by checking the house. Look for valuable personal property that should be safeguarded until you get around to obtaining a safe deposit box or vault in the name of the estate. Valuable jewels or furs, negotiable bonds in the house, or money itself cached in various and unlikely places are candidates for rescue.

As you go through the house, gather together all bank statements, tax returns, additional insurance policies you come across, credit cards, charge account cards, and bank books that you find. The documents are essential.

Once you are officially appointed executor (and surety bond has been filed unless waived as a stipulation of the will), the attorney will see that notice is properly published for the benefit of all creditors. They are all given a specific length of time, usually from four to six months, to submit all bills and statements of money owed to them by the estate. Now you can open a bank account in the name of the estate, and rent a safe deposit box or vault for the estate as well.

At this time you may have to give special attention (if it has not been done before now) to whatever income-producing assets exist that need active day-to-day management, such as an ongoing business or rental property. These may take special management.

Regarding the business, you must see to it that the present management keep it in good operation, at least until you and the estate attorney get around to looking at it more closely and deciding what is to be done with it. If it needs immediate attention, you can ask your attorney for authority to bring in a special administrator to handle its affairs.

See that account books in which the complete records of the estate can be kept are now prepared by an accountant. Then, armed with Letters Testamentary (which your lawyer has obtained from the court for you to give you authorization as executor to go into closed accounts and sealed files), you start your search to assemble the necessary records for the asset inventory.

You should realize that while the in-court appearances your attorney makes for you are comparatively short, they are vital. It is true that they are mostly routine, involving only the attorney and the judge, with no adversary present (what one writer calls "ministerial," that is, following specific rules but not necessarily requiring any particular judgment or discretion), but they are essential to the proper conduct of the probate. The bulk of the work the attorney does for the estate is outside the courtroom. Being adviser to you as executor involves legal and financial expertise that is considerable.

If the one who died had foresight, there is a folding file somewhere containing all the documents of assets or lists indicating what they are and where the supporting documents can be found. If there is no such file, however, then records of the assets must be searched out. To find these, you look into the safe deposit box or vault at the bank, talk to business partners, or check business files; visit with his or her stock broker, real estate and insurance brokers; go through everything that appear likely sources.

You need not actually *see* the property (unless it's personal property such as fine art or jewelry). If you have a deed to a lot in another part of the state where you and your spouse had been thinking of someday building a retirement home for the two of you, you don't necessarily have to go there to confirm that the lot is there. On the other hand, you *might*, if you happened to remember that the lot was bought sight unseen and the real estate company that sold it has since been indicted for selling other property on the bottom of a nearby reservoir!

The things you'll be looking for are: deeds to property, titles to houses and buildings owned jointly or separately, leases, stocks and mutual fund shares, bonds and debentures, mortgages and promissory notes receivable, life insurance naming the estate as beneficiary; business interests in corporations or partnerships; life insurance policies on others or trusts listing the one who died as beneficiary; annuities; royalties, copyrights or patents; actual cash at home or in the safe deposit box; checkbooks of checking accounts held jointly or separately; passbooks to savings accounts in banks, credit unions, or savings and loan associations; title certificates to automobiles, trucks or boats; appraisal certificates of currently possessed artwork, antiques, or valuable jewelry. If you need help in identifying any of these or recognizing them, ask your attorney to explain (even more than once, if necessary).

Check to find out if any gifts were presented within the past three years. These will have to be listed as assets of the estate for tax purposes.

If you are the spouse you will probably also be appointed guardian of the minor children. You may also be appointed custodian of their property unless the will calls for another arrangement, such as setting up a trust, with a trustee, to assume care of their property interests.

As part of assembling the assets, a separate inventory of all the debts owed to the estate must be made. You'll also have to make a special effort to collect on these debts and promissory notes outstanding. The attorney must notify the debtors that the debts are due and must be ready to sue if necessary to collect the money.

As you collect the claims of the creditors against the estate (and these are bills that were sent in routinely, not just in response to the notice as published), you'll decide which you're going to honor and which have no merit. In the will, you and the attorney may have been alerted, through a special testamentary admonition, that some claims must *not* be honored. The attorney will then prepare notices to the creditors of the rejected claims, and must be prepared to defend your refusal if any creditor disputes your decision.

The assets with no fixed value must be appraised (the business or the valuable personal property) either by an official appraiser appointed by the state or by an expert you hire yourself.

Then you must determine if any of the assets have to be sold to meet outstanding debts, or to get cash liquidity for taxes, or in order to distribute the assets that the will or court specifies must be distributed. (In many cases, according to one attorney, the liquidity problem has been highly overstated. Both the ongoing business and other sources can provide loan capital; life insurance and U.S. savings bonds with the estate as beneficiary can provide funds; and a permissive attitude on the part of the tax authorities eases the problem considerably.) However if a sale must be conducted the attorney follows through with the proper legal procedures.

Within the mandatory federal tax nine-month time limit, the attorney prepares the applicable state inheritance tax returns, state and federal income tax returns for the estate, and the federal estate tax returns. For this an accountant may have to be hired. The attorney or the accountant must also make out tax returns to cover state inheritance taxes due in other states if applicable.

Now the creditors must be paid off in a sequence of priority as required by law. The proper sequence is particularly crucial if there is question whether there will be enough assets to cover all outstanding claims. In general, the priority is in this order: the funeral expenses (up to a certain amount), the costs and expenses of administration of the estate, the family allowances, taxes, the last-illness medical and hospital bills, rents in arrears owed by the one who died, then wages and salaries due a certain number of days before death. After that, all the rest of the claims.

The attorney then prepares petitions for "instructions, authorizations, or confirmations" as required in order for the court to approve all you've done and then gets a partial or final Decree of Distribution so you can distribute the assets to the beneficiaries and heirs, which includes, parenthetically, the transferring of all assets noted in the will to be placed in trusts that go into effect at the completion of the probate.

The final step is a petition prepared for the court to discharge you as executor, thus "signing off" the estate proceed-ings. Once this is done, no one can make any subsequent claim against the estate or dispute the distribution of assets.

The time span that all this covers is usually a year at a minimum. The federal government still has three years more from the time the tax returns were submitted to audit them; according to one attorney, an executor or executrix who makes a final distribution before this audit is doing so at his or her own risk. However, for all intents and purposes, the discharge petition puts an end to the probate proceedings and your work as executor.

For anyone without extensive business and legal expertise, all these duties sound esoteric in the extreme—and perhaps they are. However, using your prerogative to call upon experts when needed and working closely with a good attorney, there is no reason at all why you shouldn't be able to handle the job as executor or executrix and do a good job.

However, as the size of the estate swells and its management and distribution problems become more and more convoluted, then professional help of the highest order is needed, probably on a continuing basis. At this point, the matter of the execution of the will slips out of this book's purview into the specialized one of the administration of very, very large estates, which cannot be treated adequately here.

Epilogue

By the time the estate has been distributed, your short-term death-related problems have melded into longer range concerns connected to your new status and not specifically pivoting on the recent death.

As the funeral and burial recede into the past, any residual expenses and loans outstanding become a part of your more general financial obligations. Insurance money not already spent or put into savings is incorporated into an overall financial program to take care of ongoing and future needs.

The estate, for all intents and purposes, has been settled. If not, whatever residual financial matters or ongoing litigation remain must be considered long range. You may have gone to work as a short-run solution to your economic or emotional problems; now these temporary goals are being replaced by more permanent career or vocational objectives.

And if the death caused a basic rupture in your life's pattern and you have moved or remarried or changed your life's direction, the future now demands your entire attention.

Just one more "coping" problem remains. If you are now

the head of a family with dependents, they are as reliant on you—and as vulnerable to your sins of omission—as you were before on the one who died.

To prevent their going through what you have just gone through, turn to Part I of this book and start preparing now for your *own* death.

Supplemental Reading Notes

For a background knowledge of my subject, I've perused many books on death and dying. Of the books I read that were clearly outside my purview, I found two particularly absorbing:

Herman Feifel, ed. *The Meaning of Death.* New York: McGraw-Hill Book Co., 1959.

Elizabeth Kubler-Ross. *On Death and Dying.* New York: Macmillan Publishing Co., 1969.

More directly in my own area of emphasis, four sociological works that I found very useful and have referred to at regular intervals are:

LeRoy Bowman. *The American Funeral: A Study in Guilt, Extravagance, and Sublimity.* Washington, D.C.: Public Affairs Press, 1959.

Robert W. Habenstein and William M. Lamers. *The History of American Funeral Directing.* Milwaukee, Wis.: Bulfin Printers, Inc., 1960.

David Sudnow. *Passing On: The Social Organization of Dying.* Englewood, N.J.: Prentice-Hall, Inc., 1969.

Glenn Vernon. *Sociology of Death: An Analysis of Death-Related Behavior.* New York: Roland Press Co., 1970.

The only book I found that directly addressed itself to the entire spectrum of pragmatic problems relating to death was a collection of essays edited by Earl A. Grollman, *Concerning Death: A Practical Guide for the Living* (Boston: Beacon Press, 1974).

In Chapter 1 the sociological description of the death ritual was adapted from Robert Blauner, "Death and Social Structure," *Psychiatry* 28(1966), pp. 378–394.

Information on burial and cremation rites was gleaned from:

Ruth Mulvey Harmer. *The High Cost of Dying.* New York: Collier Books, 1963.

Paul E. Irion. *Cremation.* Philadelphia: Fortress Press, 1963.

Maurice Lamm. *The Jewish Way in Death and Mourning.* New York: Jonathan David Publishers, 1969.

Jessica Mitford. *The American Way of Death.* Greenwich, Conn.: Fawcett Publications, Inc., 1963.

Ernest Morgan, ed. *A Manual of Death Education and Simple Burial.* Burnsville, N.C.: Celo Press, 1973.

The Price of Death: A Survey Method and Consumer Guide for Funerals, Cemeteries and Grave Markers ("Consumer Survey Handbook 3"). Seattle: Federal Trade Commission, 1975.

Glenn Vernon. *Sociology of Death.*

Information on the donation of bodies for medical research is contained in *Organ and Tissue Transplantation and Body Donation: A Compendium of Facts Compiled as an Interprofessional Source Book in Cooperation with the University of Minnesota College of Medical Sciences.* (Milwaukee: National Funeral Directors Association, 1970). This booklet sells for $5.00 and lists the requirements of 106 schools of medicine regarding such donations and also gives a summary of state laws governing body donation and the transplantation of tissues and organs. Another listing of 88 medical schools (some overlapping the 106 reprinted in the NFDA book) is in Morgan's *A Manual of Death Education and Simple Burial*, available for $1.50 from the Celo Press, Burnsville, N.C. Morgan also gives the names and addresses of places where one can write for information regarding the bequeathal of specific organs.

Information in support of the funeral and open-casket viewing is available in pamphlets from the National Funeral Directors Association:

Edgar N. Jackson. *The Significance of the Christian Funeral*, 1966.

Howard C. Raether and Robert C. Slater. *The Funeral: Facing Death as an Experience of Life*, 1974.

Paul E. Irion. *The Funeral: An Experience of Value*, 1956.

See also:

William M. Lamers, Jr. "Funerals Are Good for People— M.D.'s Included," *Medical Economics*, June 23, 1969.

Howard Raether. "The Place of the Funeral: The Role of the Funeral Director in Contemporary America." *Omega* vol. 2 (1971), pp. 136–149.

The primary source for the position of the memorial society movement is Morgan's *A Manual of Death Education*, which includes an extended question-and-answer statement by the Continental Association of Funeral and Memorial Societies, pp. 32–35.

For an opposing view see George E. LaMore, Jr. "This Will Be the Death of Us All," *Newsletter of the National Council of Teachers of English* 11 (May 1974).

For a review of British customs see Geoffrey Gorer, *Death, Grief, and Mourning in Contemporary Britain* (London: Cresset Press, 1965).

The discussion of how funeral goods and services are priced is found in both pro-funeral and anti-funeral literature. As well as Habenstein's *History of American Funeral Directing*, see:

Federal Trade Commission. *Funeral Industry Practices: A Proposed Trade Regulation Rule and Staff Memorandum*. Washington, D.C.: U.S. Government Printing Office, August 1975.

National Funeral Directors Association. "What Do You Really Know About Funeral Costs?"

For an analysis of how people view the cost of dying, see Vanderlyn R. Pine and Derek L. Phillips, "The Cost of Dying: A Sociological Analysis of Funeral Expenditures," *Social Problems* 17 (Winter 1970) pp. 405–417.

A book offering many insights into the actual nature of the funeral director—"client" relationship is Robert E. Kavanaugh, *Facing Death* (Los Angeles: Nash Publishing Co., 1972).

Brochures for the public on social security and veterans benefits can be obtained from the Social Security Administration and the Veterans' Administration, respectively.

Among the sources available on prearranging funeral and cemetery costs, and the pitfalls thereof, are:

> Association of Better Business Bureaus. *The Prearrangement and Prefinancing of Funerals: Facts You Know—Questions You Should Ask.* Reprinted in *Antitrust Aspects of the Funeral Industry,* a report of the hearings held before the Subcommittee on Antitrust and Monopoly, Committee of the Judiciary, U.S. Senate, 88th Congress, 2nd Session, re. S. Res. 252, July 7–9, 1964.

> J. T. Parnell Callahan. *Your Complete Guide to Estate Planning.* Dobbs Ferry, N.Y.: Oceana Publications, Inc., 1971.

> The Consumers Union. *Report on Life Insurance.* New York: Bantam Books, 1974.

Material on why and how to make a will is extensive; the library has a whole shelf of references. I found the following books most useful:

> Paul B. Ashley. *You and Your Will.* New York: McGraw-Hill Book Co., 1975.

> J. T. Parnell Callahan. *Your Complete Guide to Estate Planning.*

> Merle E. Dowd. *Estate Planning for Wives: A Family's Financial Guide.* Chicago: Henry Regnery Co., 1971.

> Samuel G. Kling. *The Complete Guide to Everyday Law.* New York: Pyramid Books, 1973.

> Samuel G. Kling. *Your Will and What to Do About It.* Chicago: Follett Publishing Co., 1974.

> Robert J. Schwartz. *Write Your Own Will.* New York: Collier Books, 1961.

See also:

Jacob Fisher. *Human Drama in Death Taxes.* New York: Fiduciary Publishers, Inc., 1970.

Robert Menchen. *The Last Caprice.* New York: Simon & Schuster, 1963.

In addition to the Consumers Union *Report on Life Insurance,* other sources that provide insurance information are:

Merle Dowd. *Estate Planning for Wives.*

Pennsylvania Insurance Department. *A Shopper's Guide to Life Insurance* and *A Shopper's Guide to Term Life Insurance.* Harrisburg, Pa.: State of Pennsylvania, 1972.

Gustave Simons. *Coping With Crisis.* New York: Macmillan Co., 1972.

See also: Callahan. *Your Complete Guide to Estate Planning.*

For information on probate, readers may wish to refer to Norman Dacey, *How to Avoid Probate* (New York: Crown Publishers, Inc., 1965).

Information on making final plans is contained in the advisory booklet by Virginia Lehmann, *You, the Law and Retirement* (Washington, D.C.: Dept. of Health, Education and Welfare, Sept. 1973).

For information on estate planning and trusts see Callahan, *Your Guide to Estate Planning;* Simons, *Coping With Crisis;* Ashley, *You and Your Will;* Dowd, *Estate Planning for Wives.*

In addition to Dr. Kübler-Ross's books, insight into the problems of the dying can be found in:

Nancy Doyle. *The Dying Person and the Family.* Washington, D.C.: Public Affairs Press, 1972.

Barney Glaser and Anselm Strauss. *Time for Dying.* Chicago: Aldine Publishing Co., 1968.

Bob Hale. "Some Lessons on Dying." *The Christian Century* 88 (September 1971), pp. 1076–1079.

For information on dying patients and their families, in addition to the books by Doyle, Glaser and Strauss, Kavanaugh, and Kübler-Ross, readers will find useful:

Austin Kutscher, ed. *Death and Bereavement*, Springfield, Ill.: Charles C. Thomas, 1969.

A very perceptive pamphlet covering many areas concerning death is James A. Peterson's *On Being Alone*, a National Retired Teachers Association–American Association of Retired Persons guide for widows and widowers, published in 1974.

Robert Fulton cites our having the first death-free generation in his article "The Funeral, The Funeral Director, the American Public and Its Attitude Toward Death: a 1967 Overview," in his booklet, *A Compilation of Studies of Attitudes Toward Death, Funerals, Funeral Directors*, 1971. The booklet is available from the National Funeral Directors Association.

The review of what takes place in a hospital after an expected death takes place is given in detail in David Sudnow's *Passing On: The Social Organization of Dying*.

Advice on what to watch for by way of sharp funeral-home practices when expected death takes place ("steering," refusing to release a body) is given in Bowman's *The American Funeral* and as part of the explanatory information in the FTC staff memorandum on the funeral industry's proposed trade regulation rule, among others.

For additional information on the duties of the coroner's office see Cyril H. Wecht, "The Coroner and Death" (Chapter 10 in Grollman's *Concerning Death*).

For a description of possible reactions when sudden, violent death occurs, see Robert Kavanaugh, *Facing Death*, p. 110.

For a description of what happens when one visits a funeral home, see Bowman's *The American Funeral;* Habenstein and Lamer's *History of American Funeral Directing;* and the handbook *The Price of Death: Method and Consumer Guide for Funerals, Cemeteries and Grave Markers* ("Consumer Survey Handbook 3"), put out by the Seattle regional office of the Federal Trade Commission.

The information on the burial of veterans is available in *Benefits for Veterans and Service Personnel*, Veterans' Administration pamphlet 20-67-1.

Information on nongovernmental funds to pay the funeral costs is contained in:

Sidney Margolius. *Funeral Costs and Death Benefits*. Washington, D.C.: Public Affairs Committee, 1967.

See also Dowd's *Estate Planning for Wives*.

The National Funeral Directors Association has two useful pamphlets available on making funeral arrangements: *But I Never Made Funeral Arrangements Before* and *Funeral Service: Meeting Needs, Serving People.* See also *The Funeral: Facing Death as an Experience of Life,* by Howard Raether and Robert Slater.

For information on insurance settlements, see:

"It's Important to Know Your Settlement Options." *You and Your Family.* CUNA Insurance Societies, Sept.–Oct. 1975, p. 3.

Explanations of the minimal estate and the small estate affidavit are contained in *You, the Law and Retirement,* by Virginia Lehmann, and *You and Your Will,* by Paul B. Ashley.

I refer readers desirous of further information on duties as executors of estates to the chapter in *The Last Rights: A Look at Funerals* (Owings Mills, Md.: Maryland Center for Public Broadcasting, 1974) entitled "What If You're Named Executor of an Estate," by Louise M. Brown.

Index

Accidental death, 123–137, 138
  away from home, 130–137
  in another country, 133–137
  double-indemnity insurance for,
    184
  in the home, 123–130
Administrator/administratrix, 64,
  196, 197, 198
Adopted children, 69, 72
Airlines, shipping body on, 46
American Association of University
  Women, 189
American Federation of Labor–Con-
  gress of Industrial Organiza-
  tions (AFL–CIO), 184
Amtrak, shipping body on, 46
Anniversary Masses, 173
Anniversary prayers, 175
Annuities, 69–70, 86, 193, 203
  applying for, 181–184
    company plans, 183–184
    government benefits, 183

Annuities (cont.)
    Social Security, 181–183
    union or welfare funds, 184, 185
  in financial inventory, 92
  from insurance, 186
Appraiser, 64–65, 204
Arthur Morgan School, 27
Ashes, disposing of, 13–14, 36, 99
Attorneys, 5, 84, 86, 88, 91, 92, 98, 99,
  100–102, 103, 108, 109, 161, 162
  assistance in claiming benefits,
    179–181, 185
  calling after a suicide, 140–141
  choosing, 68
  keeping name and address of, 93
  notifying after homicide, 143–144
  preparing to meet with, 69–71
  in settling estate, 190–191, 193–194,
    195, 197–206
  views on need for will, 66–67
Automobile registration, 101–102,
  204

Autopsy, 19, 116–117
  in accidental death, 127–128, 132
  in another country, 135, 136
  following suicide, 141, 142
  in homicide cases, 144
  religious attitude toward, 117, 128

Banker, keeping name and address
    of, 93
Baptismal certificate, 93
Beneficiaries. *See* Survivors
Bereavement, value of viewing body
    during, 24–25
Better Homes and Gardens, 35
Birth certificate, 76, 109
  in financial inventory, 93
Blacks, mortuaries for, 43
Black Muslims
  ban on cremation, 14
  mortuaries, 43
Body, disposing of, 8–21
  burial versus cremation, 10–19,
    147–148
  considering options, 8, 10
  description of methods, 13–14
  donating to science, 10, 19–21, 41,
    116–117, 129
  historical perspectives on, 11–13
  removal from hospital or nursing
    home, 117–118
  shipping, 46
Bonds, 55, 86, 87, 203
  in financial inventory, 92
Bronze Age, 11
Buddhism, 38
Burial, 10, 207
  in another country, 136
  arguments for, 14–15
  arrangements, 115, 200
    during terminal illness, 98–99,
      106–107
  choosing a cemetery, 48–52
  costs of, 15–16, 30–38, 121–122
  description of, 13–14
  discussing in advance, 6–7

Burial (*cont.*)
  historical perspectives on, 11–13
  letter arranging for, 41
  rites and procedures, 23–25, 28, 29,
    164–176
    memorial service, 175–176
    religious funeral, 167–175
  versus cremation, 10–19, 147–148
  See also Cemetery
Burial clothing, 32
Burial insurance. *See* Funeral
    insurance
Burial vault, 34, 59, 151, 154

Cadavers, medical use of, 10, 19–21,
    41, 117, 129
Calling hours, 168–169
Carcinoma mortality, 115
Cash, paying for funeral with, 162
Cash-value insurance, 78, 80, 81
Casket, 13, 16, 27, 33, 120, 136, 148,
    149, 152, 169
  choosing, 45, 120, 122, 150–151
  closed, 11, 43, 165, 170, 72, 174
  cost of, 13, 35, 37, 150–151
  open, 23, 24–25, 26, 28, 117, 147–
    148, 168–169, 170, 172, 174
Cemeteries, 13, 45, 128
  in another country, 136
  choosing, 48–52, 99, 153–154
  cost of lot, 37, 51, 106–107, 148–
    149, 151–152
  fees at, 37, 151–152
  lot deed in financial inventory, 93
  lot liner, 32, 34, 154
  paying for lot, 62, 163
  service at, 171, 173
  See also Burial
Charge account cards, 201–202
Charitable contributions, 78, 89
  in bequests, 65, 70
  donating deceased's belongings as,
    177–178
  in lieu of flowers, 99, 169, 172, 174
    acknowledgment of, 176

Chicago Sun-Times, 34
Children
  adopted, 69, 72
  caring for, 167
  consoling, 126, 140
  guardian for, 70, 204
  illegitimate, 69
Chinese, ancient, 11
Chinese-Americans, 38, 39
Christianity, 38, 120
  historical practices in, 12
  See also names of churches
Christian-Science, 128
  view of cremation, 17
Church committees for funeral arrangements, 120
Church of England, 16
Clergyman, 5, 126
  choosing, 45, 99, 149, 150
  fee for, 32, 37
  keeping name and address of, 93
  letter of instruction about, 41
  role at the funeral, 164–166, 170, 171, 172, 174
Closed casket, 11, 43, 165, 170, 172, 174
Clothing, disposing of deceased's, 177–178
Clubs, death and insurance benefits of, 158
Codicil, 69
Coexecutor, 68, 198, 199
Coffin. *See* Casket
Columbarium, 14, 33, 99, 151
Commendation, rite of, 173
Communion, 173
Company benefits, claiming, 179, 183–184, 185
Concrete vault, cost of, 37
Condolence calls, 166–167, 168–169, 173, 174
Consulate, contacting, 134–136
Consumers Union, 61, 75–76

Continental Association of Funeral and Memorial Societies, Inc., 26, 41, 42, 92
Coroner's office, 130, 131
  fee, 37
  investigation by, 133
    of accidental death, 125–129
    in homicide cases, 138–139, 143
    of suicide, 138–139, 141, 142
Cosmetics, in embalming, 23, 24, 25
Credit cards, 201–202
Credit unions, 92, 163
Cremation, 10, 23–25, 27, 29, 99, 117, 128
  in another country, 136
  arguments for, 15–18
  away from home, 46
  costs of, 15–16, 30–38
  description of, 13–14
  furnace for, 13
  historical perspectives, 11–13
  letter arranging for, 41
  rites and procedures, 23–25, 27, 29, 164–176
    memorial service, 175–176
    religious funeral, 167–175
  versus burial, 10–19, 147–148
Cremation societies, 12, 13, 118–119
Cremation Society of America, 13
Cremation Society of England, 12
Crypts, 13, 32, 148, 151
  cost of, 35, 149

Death, Bereavement and Mourning
  (Gorer), 28–29
Death, preparing for, 3–93
  disposition of body, 8–21
    burial versus cremation, 10–19
    considering options, 8–10
    description of methods, 13–14
    donating to science, 10, 19–21, 41
    historical perspectives, 11–13
  during terminal illness, 97–104
    disposing of property, 100–103

Death, preparing for (*cont.*)
    funeral and burial arrangements,
      98–99
    personal matters, 103–104
  funeral arrangements, 22–62, 72
    American format for, 22–24
    arguments on embalming and
      viewing, 24–25
    choices about services, 25–29
    choosing cemetery, 48–52, 99
    costs of, 25–26, 30–39, 43
    methods of pricing, 30–38
    mortuary rite, 22–29
    paying for, 53–62
    selecting a mortuary, 42–48, 98
  preliminaries, 3–7
    importance of discussion, 4, 5–7
  providing financial cushion, 75–93
    estate conservation, 85–93
    insurance, 75–84
  will, 4, 63–74, 84, 92
    advantages of, 63, 66, 67
    challenges to, 104
    compared to trusts, 89–90
    determining need for, 66–67
    making during terminal illness,
      100–101
    preliminaries to, 69–71
    standard elements, 71–73
    trusts in, 73
Death benefits funds, 53–55, 102,
    155–159
  government, 155–158
    Social Security, 20, 36, 53–54, 57,
      156–158, 163, 179
    Veterans Administration, 54, 57,
      104, 155–156, 163
  nongovernment, 158–159
    organizations and clubs, 54, 158
    unions, 54, 158–159, 187
Death certificate, 116, 117, 119, 147,
    157, 159, 181, 187
  for accidental death, 124–125, 127–
    128
  in financial inventory, 93

Death and Dying Seminar (University of Chicago), 97–98
Death notices, 32, 34, 35, 37, 45, 104,
    149, 187
Debentures in financial inventory,
    92
Decreasing renewable term insurance, 79
Decree of Distribution, 205
Dignity, standards of, 38–39
Diphtheria, 114
Divorce decree in financial inventory, 93
Doctor
  calling in case of apparent death,
    124
  keeping name and address of, 93
Documentation, importance of, 91–
    93
Double-indemnity insurance, 184
Driver's license, 132

Eastern Orthodox churches, 14
Educational trust, 90
Egyptians, ancient, 11
Embalming, 16, 19–20, 27, 33, 133,
    148, 172
  in another country, 135, 136
  arguments for and against, 24–25
  cost of, 35
  legal requirements about, 23–24
Embassy, contacting, 134–136
Employer, keeping name and address of, 93
Endowment fund costs, 32, 37
Endowment insurance, 78
Entombment, 13, 147, 148
  cost of, 35
  letter of instruction about, 41
Episcopal Church, 16
Estate, 136, 162, 178, 189, 190–206
  arranging for during terminal illness, 100–103, 107–108
  conservation of, 85–93
    avoiding probate, 86–87

Estate (*cont.*)
  importance of documentation,
    91–93
  planning program for, 87–91
  insurance in, 55, 83–84
  large, executor/executrix duties,
    196–206
  probate process, 200–206
  savings in, 55
  small, settling, 191–195
  stocks or bonds in, 55, 69–70, 86,
    87, 203
  taxes on, 68, 73, 77, 87–88, 92, 101,
    192, 194, 196, 204–205, 206
Eucharist prayer, 173
Eulogy, 99, 165, 174, 176
Evangelical denominations, 169
  ban on cremation, 14
Executor/executrix, 68, 70–71, 73,
  74, 91
  duties in settling large estate, 196–
    206
  keeping name and address of, 93
Expected death, immediate steps
  after, 116–122
Expense limit, letter of instruction
  about, 41
Ex-spouse, keeping name and address
  of, 93
Eye banks, 20

Face-value term insurance, 161
Family, death in, 113–206
  funeral arrangements, 106, 115,
    145–175, 200
    choosing a cemetery, 153–154
    conferring with mortician, 145–
      153
    paying for, 155–163, 193, 205
    rites and procedures, 164–176
  immediate steps, 116–144
    after expected death, 116–122
    after homicide, 138–139, 142–144
    following accidental death, 123–
      137, 138

Family, death in (*cont.*)
    after suicide, 138–142
  mortuary rites, 164–176
    memorial service, 175–176
    religious funeral, 166, 167–175
  postdeath arrangements, 177–189
    claiming insurance benefits, 179,
      184–189, 201
    disposing of property, 177–178
    finances, 179–184
  settling estates, 190–206
    large, 196–206
    small, 190–195
  when imminent, 105–109
    funeral and burial arrangements,
      106–107
    making a will, 107–108
Family allowance, 197
Family lot, 49, 154
Federal estate tax, 92, 101, 205
Federal Trade Commission (FTC),
  33, 34, 147, 148, 150
Federated Funeral Directors of
  America, 34
Finances, postdeath arrangements
  for, 179–184
  annuity payments, 181–184
  company plans, 183–184
  government programs and
    Social Security, 181–183
  union and welfare funds, 184
  funds immediately available,
    180–181
  joint bank accounts, 179,
    180–181
  loans, 181
  savings bonds, 181
Financial cushion, providing, 75–93
  estate conservation, 85–93
  avoiding probate, 86–87
  documentation in, 91–93
  planning program for, 87–91
  insurance, 75–84
  life, 77–84

Financial cushion, providing (*cont.*)
  Social Security (OASDI),
    75–76
  when death is imminent, 100–103
Fire department, 124, 125
First aid, calling for, 124
Flowers, 43–44, 165
  acknowledgment of, 176
  choosing, 45, 99, 149, 150
  cost of, 32, 37
  memorial gift in lieu of, 99, 169,
    172, 174
Foreign country, death in, 133–137
Fraternal clubs, death benefits and
    insurance of, 54, 158, 187
Fraternal organization rituals, 45,
    149
Fringe-benefit trust, 90
Fulton, Robert, 113, 121–122
Fundamentalist sects, 14
Funeral arrangements, 22–62, 72,
    106, 115, 145–175, 200
  in accidental death, 129–130,
    132–133
  after medical use of corpse, 20,
    21
  choosing a cemetery, 48–52, 90,
    153–154
  conferring with mortician,
    145–153
  costs of, 25–26, 30–39, 43, 106–107,
    121–122
    burial versus cremation, 15–16
    caskets, 13, 35, 37, 150–151
    cemetery lot, 37, 51, 106–107,
      148–149, 151–152
    deciding what to spend, 38–39,
      151–152
    methods of pricing, 30–38
    during terminal illness, 98–99,
      106–107
  need to discuss plans, 4, 6–7
  paying for, 53–62, 155–163, 193, 205
    by cash, 162

Funeral arrangements (*cont.*)
  death benefit funds, 53–55, 102,
    155–159
  "other arrangements" for,
    162–163
    by prepayment, 55–62, 159–161
    with savings, 56, 161–162
  rites and procedures, 22–29,
    164–176
    American format of, 22–24
    choices about services, 25–29,
      164–176
    embalming and viewing, 24–25
    memorial service, 175–176
    religious, 167–175
  selecting a mortuary, 42–48, 98,
    118, 119–120, 121
Funeral directors and funeral homes.
  See Morticians and mortuaries
Funeral Directors Services Associa-
    tion of Greater Chicago, 34
Funeral insurance, 60–61, 160–161
Funeral societies, 98, 118–119

Garnishments, 163
Gift tax exemptions, 89
Gorer, Geoffrey, 28–29
Government death benefits, 155–158,
    183
  Social Security, 20, 36, 53–54, 57,
    156–158, 163, 179
  Veterans Administration, 54, 57,
    104, 155–156, 163
Grave liner, 32, 34, 154
Grave markers, 16, 32, 33, 34, 37, 51,
    152, 154, 163
  dedication of (Jewish), 175
Graveside service, 171
Greece, ancient, 12
Group life insurance, 81–83
  claiming benefits, 185, 188–189
  on-the-job, 82
  pension trust, 82
  in special-interest groups, 83, 187

Guardian, for minor children, 70, 204

Hand, Learned, 88
Health records, 93
Heart attacks, 115
Heirs. *See* Survivors
Holographic wills, 67
Home, death in, 123–130
Homicide, 138–139, 142–144
  coroner's investigation of, 138, 143
Homily, 173
Honorarium, clergyman's, 32, 37
Hospital, removal of body from, 117–118
Humanist service, 170
Hymns, instruction about, 41

Inheritance taxes, 68, 73, 77, 87–88, 92, 101, 192, 194, 196, 204–205, 206
Illegitimate children, 69
Immediate steps, 116–144
  in case of accidental death, 123–127, 138
  in another country, 133–137
  away from home, 130–137
  in the home, 123–130
  in case of expected death, 116–122
  in case of homicide, 138–139, 142–144
  in case of suicide, 138–142
Income tax return, 76, 91, 101, 178, 201–202, 205
Income-splitting devices, 87, 90
Industrial insurance. *See* Funeral insurance
Inflation, effect on equity, 87
Influenza, 114
Inheritance statutes, 114
Inheritance tax. *See* Taxes, estate
Inquest, 142
Installment plan, 162
Institute of Electrical and Electronics Engineers, 189

Insurance, 4, 73, 75–84, 85, 89, 98, 101, 108, 136, 149, 160–161, 162, 178, 193, 201–202, 207
  claiming benefits, 179, 184–189, 201
  group term, 185, 188–189
  options in, 186–188
  using a broker, 185–186
  in financial inventory, 92
  getting during terminal illness, 102–103
  "industrial" for funeral, 60–61, 160–161
  life, 66, 69–70, 77–84, 86, 193, 203, 205
    as death-benefit protection, 77–78
    as estate-building device, 55, 83–84
    in financial inventory, 92
    getting during terminal illness, 102
    group, 81–83
    Social Security, 75–76
    term, 78, 79–81, 161
    tips, 83
  renewable term, 56–57, 79
  Social Security (OASDI), 75–76
  in suicide cases, 139, 142
Insurance agent or broker, 5, 88, 161, 203
  claiming benefits through, 185–186
  keeping name and address of, 93
Insurance trust, 90
Inter vivos (living) trust, 87, 89–90
Inventory, financial, 91–93
Irion, Paul, 25, 170

Joint bank account, 59–60
  getting funds from, 179, 180–181
Joint tenancy, 178, 193
Judaism, 11, 12
  attitude toward autopsy, 117
  cemeteries, 48
  funeral practices, 173–175

Judaism (*cont.*)
  at the cemetery, 174
  congregational committee for
    arrangements, 120–121
  period of mourning, 174–175
  preparation of the body, 173
  service, 174
  mortuaries, 42–43
  view of cremation, 15, 17

Kavanaugh, Robert, 44, 139–140
KCET (television station), 35
Kübler-Ross, Elizabeth, 24–25

LaMore, George E., Jr., 27
Lawyers. *See* Attorneys
Letter of Instructions, 40–41, 45,
  99
Letters Testamentary, 202
Level renewable term insurance, 79
Liabilities, in financial inventory,
  92
Life insurance, 66, 69–70, 77–84, 86,
  193, 203, 205
  claiming benefits, 179, 184–189,
    201
    group term, 185, 188–189
    options in, 186–188
    using a broker, 185–186
  as death-benefit protection, 77–78
  as an estate-building device, 55,
    83–84
  in financial inventory, 92
  getting during terminal illness,
    102
  group, 81–83
    on-the-job, 82
    pension trust, 82
    in special-interest group, 83, 187
  Social Security, 75–76
  term, 78, 79–81, 161
    decreasing renewable, 79
    level renewable, 79
  tips, 83
Limited-payment life insurance, 78

Living (*inter vivos*) trust, 87, 89–90
Loans, 77, 91, 181
Lodge rituals, 45, 168, 172
Lodges, insurance and death
  benefits of, 54, 158, 187
Los Angeles County Coroner, 126,
  143
Los Angeles Times, 33–34, 35
Lot liner, cemetery, 32, 34, 154
Lutheran Burial Association, 120
Lutheran Church, Missouri Synod,
  14
Lying in state, 168–169

*Manual of Death Education and
  Simple Burial, A* (Morgan),
  17–18, 27
Marriage certificate, 76, 108
  in financial inventory, 93
Maryland Center for Public
  Broadcasting, 34–35
Mass, funeral, 172–173
Mausoleums, 13, 30, 32, 151
Medical bills, 106
Medical examiners. *See* Coroner's
  office
Medical insurance policies, 185
Medical science, donating body to,
  10, 19–21, 41, 116–117, 129
Memorial gifts, 99, 169, 172, 174,
  176
  acknowledgment of, 176
Memorial reception, 169
Memorial record, 44–45
Memorial service, 16, 23, 171, 175–
  176
  arguments for and against, 25–29
  without viewing, 11
Memorial service movement, 25–26,
  28
Memorial societies, 16, 17, 41, 42,
  98, 106
  charges, 36
Memorial stone, 16, 32, 33, 34, 37,
  152, 154, 163

Military records, 76, 93, 109
Ministers. *See* Clergyman
Monthly installments, from insurance, 186
Month's Mass, 173
Morgan, Ernest, 17–18, 27
Morgue, 118, 128, 131, 133, 141, 144, 148
Mormon Church, 15
Mortgages, 69–70
    in financial inventory, 92
Morticians and mortuaries, 20, 99, 106, 128, 131, 187
    affiliated with memorial service movement, 26, 36
    arranging prepayment with, 57–61, 159–161
    choosing, 42–48, 98, 118, 119–120, 121
    conferring with, 145–153
    cost of, 25–26, 30–39, 43, 106–107, 121–122
    methods of pricing, 30–38
    notifying of death, 117–118
    price list, 42
    recommendation of cemetery, 49
    release for, 117
    removal of body by, 141, 144
    views on embalming, 24
Mortuary card, carrying, 45–46
Mortuary rites, 22–29, 164–176
    deciding on type of service, 25–29
    embalming and viewing, 24–25
    memorial service, 175–176
    religious funeral, 166, 167–175
        Jewish, 173–175
        Protestant, 22, 168–171
        Roman Catholic, 171–173
Mourning, 177
    Jewish period of, 174–175
    value of, 29
Multiple trust, 90
Mummification of memories, 178
Music, 34, 169, 173, 176
    letter of instruction about, 41

Music (*cont.*)
    selecting, 45, 99, 149, 150
Mutual-fund shares, 203
    in financial inventory, 92

Najarian, John, 21
Names and addresses, making list of, 93, 102
National cemeteries. *See* Veterans' cemeteries
National Funeral Directors Association (NFDA), 34, 59, 152
National Kidney Foundation, 20
Naturalization papers, 93
New York Cremation Society, 12–13
Newspaper death notices, 32, 34, 35, 45, 104, 149, 187
    cost of, 37
Nongovernment death benefits, 158–159
    organizations and clubs, 54, 158–159, 187
    unions, 54, 158–159, 187
Nonsectarian funeral homes, 42
Nuncupative wills, 67
Nursing home, removal of body from, 117–118

Obituary notice, 32, 34, 35, 37, 45, 104, 149, 187
Old Age, Survivors' and Disability Insurance (OASDI), 75–76
On-the-job group life insurance, 82
Open-casket viewing, 26, 28, 147–148
    after autopsy, 117
    arguments for and against, 24–25, 43
    embalming for, 23
    memorial service without, 11
    at Protestant funeral, 168–169
Organ transplants, 19–21
Organ-collection foundations, 20

Organizations, death benefits of, 54, 158, 187
Orphans court, 64
Out-of-town death, 130–137
  in another country, 133–137

Pallbearers, choosing, 149, 150
Paramedics, 124
Passport, in financial inventory, 93
Pension benefits, 82, 85, 86, 89, 193
  claiming, 179, 183–184, 185
  in financial inventory, 92
Pentecostal groups, 169
Personal loan, 91
Personal property, 69–70, 86, 177, 190, 194, 201, 203
  in financial inventory, 92
Phillips, D. L., 39
Picasso, Pablo, 63
Pine, V. R., 39
Pneumonia, 115
Police, 131
  action after accident, 124–125, 127
  investigation of homicide, 142–144
  in suicide case, 139, 141
Poliomyelitis, 114
Postdeath arrangements, 177–189
  claiming insurance benefits, 179, 184–189, 201
    group term, 185, 188–189
    options in, 186–188
    using a broker, 185–186
  disposing of personal property, 177–178
  finances, 179–184
    annuity payments, 181–184
    funds immediately available, 180–181
Prepayment, funeral and burial costs, 55–62, 159–161
  for burial, 62
  with renewable term insurance, 56–57

Prepayment (*cont.*)
  savings account for, 56, 161–162
  for specific mortuary, 57–61, 159–161
Probate, 5, 64, 89–90, 91, 104, 162, 180
  avoiding, 86–87
  filing will for, 190, 200
  large estate in, 196–206
  process, 200–206
  small estate in, 191–195
Professional group insurance, claiming, 185–186
Profit-sharing plans, 89, 93
  claiming on, 179, 183–184, 185
Protestantism, 175
  funeral ceremony, 22, 168–171
    at the cemetery, 171
    service, 169–170
    viewing the body, 168–169
  funeral homes, 42
  view of cremation, 15, 16
  See also names of churches
"Putting My House in Order" (Continental Association of Funeral Homes), 92

Rabbi, 174
Railroad Retirement Act, 54
Railroads, shipping body on, 46
Real estate agents, 203
Real property (real estate), 69–70, 86, 87, 89, 108, 190, 194
  in financial inventory, 92
  letter of instruction about, 41
Religion, 11, 114, 164
  and attitude toward autopsy, 117, 128
  as basis for choosing cemetery, 48, 153
  favoring of burial in, 14–15
  in funeral rituals, 22, 28, 166, 167–175
    Jewish, 173–175
    Protestant, 22, 168–171

Religion (*cont.*)
  Roman Catholic, 171–173
  selecting mortuaries on basis of,
    42–43, 121
  stand on medical use of corpse,
    20, 21
  view of cremation, 16–18
  See also names of religions
Religious memorial service, 170
Remarriage, 6
Renewable term insurance, 56–57,
  79
Resuscitation unit, 124
Retirement home, 6
Retirement income, 77, 79
Roman Catholic
  cemeteries, 48
  funeral, 171–173
    at the cemetery, 173
    Mass, 172–173
    wake, 172
  funeral homes, 42
  view of cremation, 15
Romans, ancient, 12

Safe deposit box, 100, 102, 106, 190,
  191, 201, 202, 203
Savings accounts, 78, 101, 108, 203
  in estate, 55
  in financial inventory, 92
  for funeral expenses, 56, 161–162
Science, donating body to, 10, 19–
  21, 41, 116–117, 129
Sea, burial at, 10
Second Vatican Council (1963), 15
Securities. *See* Stocks and bonds
Sepulchre, 11
Shiva, 174–175
Shock, 126, 130
Small face-value term insurance,
  161
Social clubs, insurance and death
  benefits of, 158
Social Security, 45, 85, 162, 189,
  193

Social Security (*cont.*)
  applying for benefits, 179, 181–
    183
  card in financial inventory, 93
  insurance (OASDI), 75–76
  keeping name and address of
    office, 93
  lump-sum death benefit, 20, 36,
    53–54, 57, 156–158, 163, 179
Sprinkling trust, 90
Standard adult funeral, cost of, 30–
  38
State inheritance tax, 205
Stepchildren, 69
Stock broker, 93, 203
Stocks and bonds, 55, 69–70, 86, 87,
  100, 108, 203
  in financial inventory, 92
Stone Age, 11
Suicide, 108, 138–142
  coroner's investigation of, 138–
    139, 141, 142
Surety bond, 198, 202
Surrogate court, 64
Survivors, 6, 22, 30, 36, 37, 84
  advantage of will for, 63–66, 67
  collecting prepaid funeral ex-
    penses, 57–58, 159–161
  consulting services for, 31
  financial cushion for, 75–93
    estate conservation, 85–93
    insurance, 75–84
    when death is imminent, 100–
      103
  list of names and addresses for,
    93
  notifying of death, 200
  remarriage, 6
  value of viewing body for, 24–25
  See also Family, death in
Sympathy cards, 174

Tax attorney, 84, 86, 88
Tax returns, 76, 91, 101, 178, 201–
  202, 205

Taxes, estate, 68, 73, 77, 87–88, 92, 101, 192, 194, 196, 204–205, 206
Television, 113
Term insurance, 78, 79–81, 161
  claiming, 185–186, 188–189
  renewable, 56–57, 79
Terminal illness, preparations during, 97–109
  disposing of property, 100–103, 107–108
    financial, 101–102
    insurance, 102–103
    making a will, 100–101, 107–108
  for funeral and burial, 98–99, 106–107
  personal matters, 103–104
Testamentary trusts, 73, 89, 90
Time-payment contract, 58–59
Transportation costs, 32
Travelers' insurance, 184
Trusts, 4, 68, 87, 88–89, 101, 203
  compared to will, 89–90
  educational, 91
  set up in wills, 73
  for survivors, 84, 204
Truth-in-lending laws, 163
Twenty-third Psalm, 174

Uniform Anatomical Gift Act, 19, 20
Uniform Donor Cards, 20–21, 41
Uniform Probate Code, 192
Unions, 172
  claiming pension, 184, 185
  death benefits, 54, 93, 158–159
  keeping name and address of, 93
  welfare plan, 85
Unitarian/Universalist Church, 17
U.S. Navy, 10
U.S. Savings Bonds, 86, 102, 193, 205
  cashing by beneficiary, 181
U.S. Senate, 158–159
U.S. State Department, 136–137

U.S. Supreme Court, 182–183
University of Chicago, 97
University of Minnesota Hospitals, 21
Urn, for ashes, 14

Veterans Administration, 149, 162
  death benefits, 54, 57, 104, 155–156, 163
    claiming, 179
  keeping name and address of office, 93
Veterans' cemeteries, 45–46, 149, 155–156
Victoria, Queen, 12
Viewing the body, 26, 147–148
  after autopsy, 117
  arguments for and against, 24–25, 43
  embalming for, 23
  memorial service without, 11
  at Protestant funeral, 168–169
Visitors' book, 169, 172

Wake, 172
Welfare funds, claiming, 184
Whooping cough, 114
Wills, 4, 63–74, 84, 92, 106, 192, 194–195
  advantages of, 63–66, 67
  challenges to, 104
  compared to trusts, 89–90
  determining need for, 66–67
  filing for probate, 190, 200
  for large estate, 196–201, 204, 206
  making during terminal illness, 100–101, 107–108
  preliminaries to, 69–71
  standard elements in, 71–73
  trusts in, 73
World War I, 104
World War II, 12
Writers Guild of America, 189
W-2 form, 76